UNMASKED

Demons lurking behind psychological symptoms

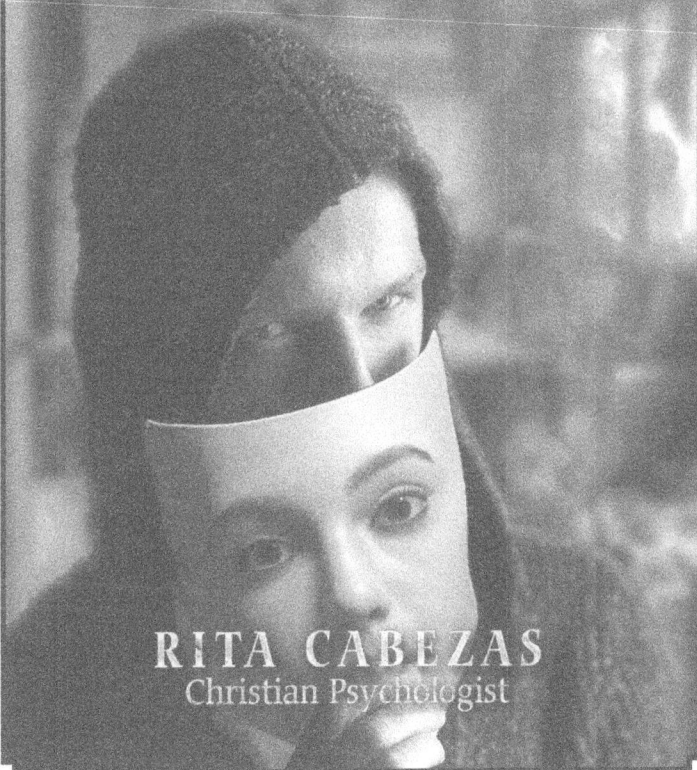

RITA CABEZAS
Christian Psychologist

Originally self-published in Spanish as *Desenmascarado*
©1986 by Rita Cabezas
Published as *Desenmascarado*,

©1988 by Rita Cabezas
Editorial Unilit, Miami, Fl. 33172
ISBN 0-945792-04-2
Product # 490239

There have been three editions of the Spanish version.
Translated by Elizabeth M. Lewis
Jacket and interior design by Jannio Monge
English version: UNMASKED Demons lurking behind psychological symptoms

© 2020 by Rita Cabezas
KINDLE ebook in Amazon

ISBN: 9780578753850

RITA CABEZAS

Christian psychologist, minister, author and speaker.

Private practice in Costa Rica.

Office phone number: (506) 2273-1245.

Office address: San Ramón de Tres Ríos, 300 meters east of Catholic
Church, next to Pupitres MUDAMISA.

For appointments and speaking invitations, send a message to WhatsApp
+1 506-8682-4450.

Email: ritacabezas.org@gmail.com

Messenger: ritacabezas.39

https://www.facebook.com/rita.cabezas.39

YouTube: RitaCabezasOFICIAL

TABLE OF CONTENTS

DEDICATION

I dedicate the English version of this book to my oldest son, Santiago, who did not stop pressuring me into getting my first book, Desenmascarado, translated into English.

I published Desenmascarado, the Spanish version of Unmasked, when I was 23. I am now 67. It took me all these years to finally get this job done. I'm sure Satan was congratulating himself on having sidetracked me for good and that it would never be published in English, but God used Santiago to make it happen.

Thank you, Santiago, for not giving up on this project until it was completed! This just goes to show that we all require a bit of nagging on the part of those who love us in order to achieve the goals we keep putting off.

FOREWORD

S atan masks his presence in many ways. God has been working through Rita for a number of years, showing her many of his disguises that are relevant to her professional practice. She offers this book to share her experiences in a remarkable adventure that has set her face to face with the Evil One himself in a towering spiritual battle. It is a battle that few have dared to wage so openly.

Rita has been slowly opening doors that had remained closed to Christians for centuries. She has found that the key for opening them is the name of Jesus, the name above all names before which every knee will bow.

Rita, as a professional psychologist, has succeeded in combining her scientific background with research in the field of the demonic – a field that appears to be intangible but is absolutely real to those who have experienced it. She has applied the tools of psychology to the practice of spiritual deliverance, thus revealing the complex, little understood relationship between the psychological and the spiritual.

Her pioneering work has unquestionably led her into virgin territory in the behavioral sciences. Psychology had always been reluctant to delve into this unknown dimension, despite its undeniable role in the scope of human conduct.

We have known Rita for years and have sat in on many of her deliverance sessions. We have witnessed her methodology first-hand and have observed the practices she describes in this book. All the cases we have experienced have led to positive outcomes, some with astonishing speed, and others through slower and more laborious processes.

We personally know many who have been received healing and deliverance through her work. We can corroborate the lasting results of her treatment in spiritual deliverance, results that cannot be shunted aside as a fleeting by-product of hysteria.

We agree with her that people oppressed by demonic powers will never find genuine relief through merely medical, psychiatric or psychological treatment if Jesus Christ is left out.

This book is a call to other Christians in the healing professions; we urge them to get involved in this battle between spiritual powers, because people suffering from the physical and psychological effects of demonic attack will turn specifically to them for help. This task, delegated to the followers of Jesus Christ who sent his disciples to heal the sick and free the captives, is a clear continuation of his ministry.

George and Gayle Weinand

Missionaries to Costa Rica

Calvary Chapel Ministries

This book introduces a form of deliverance therapy that has produced excellent results. One of the most striking cases I have seen involved a twelve-year old boy. I was praying for him one day when a demon began speaking through the child's mouth, even though I had said nothing about demons. I had not even suspected the presence of demons. When I asked its name, it answered: "Theft." I cast it out in Jesus' name, but then a second demon manifested and called itself "Escape." They both left. I believe the child was not even aware of what was happening, and in the end he opened his eyes and asked if I had finished praying for him, as if nothing out of the ordinary had occurred.

This was two years ago. The boy had a recurring history of theft and frequently escaped from the institution where he lived. He had most recently stolen fifty thousand colones, buried the money along with stolen objects, and was planning to run away to Panama. The caregivers discovered his plan and found the money.

Since the day of his deliverance, he has made no further attempts to run away or steal. Institution staff can confirm this as a fact.

It was my first experience in this field and was something I had never even considered. It simply happened. I have since had more opportunities to practice what I learned about casting out demons, and I can testify that it is an effective means of eliminating symptoms that behavioral science classifies as strictly psychological. Having lived through these experiences, I can conclude that they are more of a spiritual nature. I have sat in on many of Rita's deliverance sessions. The events that take place in these treatments shift from the psychological realm into the spiritual, but both are clearly present. The manifestation phase is characterized by sudden personality changes, including alterations of behavior, gestures, tone of voice, language and body movements that are evident to anyone watching and that might suggest a diagnosis of multiple personality disorder or dissociative disorder. I am a Christian psychologist, however, and I firmly believe that the phenomena I have witnessed cannot be properly explained within a limited psychological framework. I am convinced that the spiritual world exists, and if we as psychologists hope to improve the overall health of the people we treat, we must include the spiritual dimension in their treatment.

Margarita Alvarado
Psychologist
University of Costa Rica

I have accompanied Rita in many of her experiences with spiritual deliverance. I can testify to the fact that the results are long-lasting. One of the patients I witnessed was a woman who was such a heavy smoker that she averaged eighty cigarettes a day. We led her through a process of inner healing and deliverance, and she was able to quit smoking completely and permanently. I continued to monitor this patient for two years and can safely say that she never resumed smoking.

I also took part in the deliverance of a psychologist who, due to certain events in her life, seemed to have developed two personalities. However, it became evident over the course of treatment that the destructive personality manifesting in her was not in fact a second personality, but rather a demon. This patient went through three deliverance sessions and achieved striking changes. Her psychological and spiritual state continue to be stable a year and a half later. Her friends and acquaintances are unaware that she was involved in deliverance from demonic influence, but they have noticed and commented on that fact that she is changed. I know her personally and professionally and can attest to the fact that her transformation is very evident and has remained.

I too have gone through the type of treatment described in this book. My case required only a single two-hour session that resolved a number of problems I had been experiencing in my life, and they have never bothered me again. I must emphasize that this form of healing cannot be practiced by a non-Christian therapist because the power that produces deliverance does not come from the practitioner, but from God himself. Only those who have surrendered their own lives to God can serve as instruments of his power, so I again insist that this type of treatment can be administered only by a believing Christian.

Celita Ulate
Psychologist
University of Costa Rica

The evidence is clear and irrefutable: Satan's oppression in the lives of Christians is a reality, even for the most sincere and dedicated children of God. We know this through personal experience. The masked enemy of all Christians can wreak havoc in a person's life and family, so he must be unmasked and bound, cast out and his chains broken in the name of Jesus Christ, just as the Bible teaches us to do.

God has given spiritual gifts to his church, and they need to be put to use in ministries such as this. The church of Jesus Christ could become much more powerful, active and effective if Christian leaders would take this part of the Gospel more seriously and begin to "set the captives free."

This is the intention of Rita Cabezas' book UNMASKED. It describes her experiences and examines her conclusions in light of the Bible, that they might serve as a starting point for all those who are called by God to devote their lives to this much-needed work of Christian ministry.

Readers who truly wish to profit from this fascinating book must approach it with an open mind and a heart willing to learn whatever God is teaching.

Román Giménez

PhD in Ministry

Fuller Theological Seminary

Ordained Minister, Presbyterian Church of the USA

Marriage and Family Counselor

Sandra Giménez

MA in Theology

Fuller Theological Seminary

Youth Counselor

PREFACE

Many people believe that the practice of spiritual deliverance is the exclusive domain of Christian clergy and missionaries. In my view, it belongs in the hands of every truly committed Christian. Jesus sent his disciples to heal the sick and set the captives free.

Health professionals need to become fully knowledgeable about the scientific masks the devil uses, because demon-tormented people turn to them for help. A passage from Mark 5:1-20 tells the story of a demon-possessed man from the Gadarenes. If he lived today, who would he ask for help, if not a physician, psychologist or psychiatrist?

Demons of every kind are at work. They can invade the body, inflicting it with infirmity, pain, blindness, muteness, cancer, gluttony, asthma, coughing, epilepsy, fatigue and vice, and Christian health workers are equipped to detect them in patients. They also invade the mind and emotions, which they can inflict with nervousness, anxiety, anguish, depression, discouragement, insanity, jealousy, self-contempt, insecurity, suicidal impulses and fear, and it takes a Christian psychiatrist, psychologist or counselor to discern them. We are the ones, and I speak as a Christian psychologist, equipped to see through the many clever disguises Satan has come up with to clothe himself in the robes of science, standing as a modern version of the age-old angel of light in this day and age when science reigns supreme.

Clergy also need to work with all who come for help, but nowadays very few people associate physical or psychological ailments with the spiritual world. Unfortunately, most clergy do not know how to recognize bondage or set the captives free. They too have fallen prey to scientific rationalism, promptly turning to "proper" health professionals for the occasional deluded sufferers who are so simple-minded as to ascribe their afflictions to spiritual causes.

This book is my call to Christian health professionals to start building up their gifts of spiritual discernment. Even those who feel they lack such a gift can request it of God, who freely gives. He is eager for all his children to desire it and receive it.

We cannot avoid contact with demons. We run up against them all the time in our offices and clinics, disguised as physical, mental and emotional illnesses. We see so many stubbornly persistent symptoms refusing to let go, and it would behoove us to understand who the true culprits are. The fact is that demons will never succumb to psychiatric drugs, straitjackets or electroshock. They yield only to a Christian who stands up to them in Jesus' name.

This claim could be easily misconstrued: I do not claim that demons are lurking behind every symptom. Such an assertion would be dreadfully wrong, but I do believe they often have a hand in the most stubborn symptoms. All too often, when science falls short and settles on a label such as "incurable" or "hopeless," healing can be found in the name of Jesus.

I was 20 years old when I began to discover that Satan was crouching behind so many physical and psychological symptoms. I decided to help unmask him and show him for who he is: a destructive spirit who commands legions of lesser demons.

In a moment of solitude I assured him that I would put on the whole armor that God has given his children and would fight him for as long as God gave me life, not with human weapons but "with the power of God able to destroy strongholds." No sooner had I uttered that declaration in the spirit realm, than demon-tormented sufferers began coming into my office. I never had to go looking for them because God himself led them to me. This was how he confirmed that I was truly doing his work.

When I first wrote this book in Spanish in 1987, my battle was just beginning. I have learned much along the way, and I know there is much more I have yet to discover about the spirit realm. Those who persist in this battle will never finish learning about spiritual warfare or complete their training under Jesus, our Conqueror, Jehovah, Lord of Heavenly Hosts and our Powerful Holy Spirit. I have had to wage my own personal battles against the kingdom of darkness as well, and I know I am not yet finished. In all of it, I have personally experienced that "God is our refuge and strength, an ever-present help in trouble" (Ps 46:1). The Bible promises that the devil will flee if you submit your life to God and resist him, and I am living proof that this is true. I challenge you to test it for yourself and to ask God for the tools you will need to discover it.

"Whoever has ears, let them hear what the Spirit says to the churches." (Rev 3:13). I will be content if the things I have written here provide some guidance to others who choose to follow a similar path. If these pages contain any truth at all, the credit must go to God himself. The mistakes are mine alone.

BIOGRAPHICAL NOTE FROM THE AUTHOR

I was born in Philadelphia, Pennsylvania when my Costa Rican father, studying medicine in the USA, met and eventually married my American mother. I was five years old when we came to live in Costa Rica, where I grew up. I went to the USA for my university studies, first at Greenville College in Illinois, a Free Methodist college, and finally at the University of South Florida in Tampa, where I completed my BA in psychology. I then did some graduate work at Florida Tech University in Orlando.

Upon my return home to Costa Rica, I took courses in theology at the Seminario Bíblico Latinoamericano. I completed my degree studies with a Licenciatura in psychology from the Universidad de Costa Rica, where I wrote the first thesis in the field of Psychology of Religion in Costa Rica,

Disposiciones Religiosas y su Influencia sobre el Ejercicio de la Profesión del Psicólogo (How Religious Beliefs Influence Psychologists in their Professional Practice).

I opened my private practice in San José and have been providing psychological counseling since 1980. I published my first two books, Desenmascarado (Editorial Unilit) and Psicoterapia Cristiana (Libros CLIE), in 1988.

I have been involved in Christian ministry since age thirteen, serving as a Sunday School teacher, Christian camp leader and church youth group leader. My professional counseling has always been from a biblical perspective, combining God's power released through prayer and spiritual gifts with scientific knowledge of psychology.

I founded a church in Costa Rica, Iglesia Libertad, which grew out of my private practice in Christian psychotherapy. I pastored this church for twelve years and turned it over to another pastor when I began to travel internationally for speaking engagements to teach and minister in the areas of inner healing, development of prophetic gifting, personal and territorial deliverance and confrontation of demonic principalities.

I published two more books with Editorial Unilit: Guía de Liberación de Influencia Demoníaca por medio de la Palabra (1993) and Lucha Contra

Principados Demoníacos (1995) which I first self-published in English in 1992 under the title Struggling Against Demonic Principalities. I have also self-published twenty-six books to use with my clients and in my teaching seminars. Just recently, I have started publishing ebooks for Kindle to sell through Amazon: Arrebata Tu Sanidad, Libérate del Temor, Defeating Demonic Principalities.

I continue with my private practice in Costa Rica and treat people from many countries by videocall. In addition, my international travel sometimes provides me the opportunity to offer Christian psychotherapy services to people there.

All the names and personal identifying information on the people whose cases are discussed in this book have been changed to protect their privacy.

The only exception is Gean Carlo (chapter 12), who was willing to be identified, to glorify God through his testimony.

CHAPTER 1

EUGENIA: THE DEMONIZED STUDENT

"I need to talk to someone about this," she said fearfully. There is no one else I can turn to. Maybe you won't even believe me, but at least I know I can trust you."

"I'll try to help," I assured the frightened teenager, and encouraged her to go on. "Tell me everything you want to say, and we can figure it out together."

"When people come into my room, they always get a chill up their spine. It's very strange," she said, "and my room smells funny. I have horrible dreams all the time, nightmares that are so real, it seems like they are actually happening. Last night when I was asleep, the bed started shaking all by itself. It wouldn't stop moving! All of a sudden, I heard two voices having a big fight. I didn't understand their language, but I knew they were fighting over me. I was very scared. It seemed like they were God and Satan arguing over who I belonged to."

Eugenia was a young student, seventeen years old. She was visibly concerned that I would think she was "crazy," but after observing her and listening to her, I could clearly see that she was not. It was obvious, though, that she had been terrified by a string of recent supernatural experiences.

As we spoke at greater length, I began to identify Eugenia's psychological problems. She had been raped by her uncle at age four. Her family had decided to ignore the whole episode, and it became a taboo subject. Nobody ever spoke to Eugenia about it. They apparently felt that she had been too young to have a clear awareness of what was happening and would forget about it as she grew. Now, however, the consequences of this early sexual abuse were starting to show up. Even as the other girls in her class began talking about their first boyfriends, she felt a strong emotional barrier between herself and the young men. Several boys had shown an interest in her, and she liked them too; but every time one of them came too close and tried to put his arm around her or hold her hand, she was overcome by a mixture of fear and revulsion. She would leap up and run away. Eugenia knew this was not normal behavior and was desperate to get over it.

One of her recurring nightmares found her with a young man who was her boyfriend. When he tried to kiss her, she would open her eyes and his face would be transformed into that of a woman cackling with glee over the trick she had played. Eugenia would wake up drenched in sweat, feeling the same mixture of fear and revulsion that she often experienced in the presence of men.

I offered my assistance with her emotional problems, but I also explained that I had no experience with the kinds of supernatural phenomena she had described at the outset. I told her that someone else would have to help her with that specific part of her problem. The girl commented that a close relative had been having strange experiences like hers, had gone to a Christian minister for prayers of spiritual deliverance, and had been greatly relieved. Eugenia decided to look up the same minister for help with the spiritual dimension of her own problems.

The next week, she reported that she had attended a three-hour session with the minister, and four demons had spoken through her mouth and been expelled. This was very new to me, and I urged her to describe the whole experience in detail.

"The minister," replied Eugenia, "walked me through some Bible passages about how Jesus had come to Earth to destroy the works of the

Devil and set us free from his influence. He also told me that every person who believes in Jesus as the Son of God has the power to stand up to Satan and his demons. First he prayed and then started commanding the demons in me to say their names. My mouth started moving on its own, and I could hear everything it was saying but I had no control over it. I was fully aware of what was happening, but I was powerless to intervene. It was as if I were a spectator in my own body.

"Several times I tried to speak up," Eugenia continued, "but I couldn't because this other personality was using my mouth. At one point I experienced feelings of terrible fury at the minister. I wanted to tear him apart! But it couldn't really have been me, because I had no reason to be angry with him. It was that force in me that hated him. My body threw itself at him and began to hit him and pull his hair. I tried to stop myself, but I couldn't control my body. It was so embarrassing! The minister held my arm tightly and ordered the demon to be still and to let me sit down. So I sat. I was aware of my own feelings, but at the same time, I could actually sense what the demon was feeling. It was very weird!

"When the demon spoke, it referred to me as someone else separate from itself. It said it was giving me the recurring nightmares. When the minister asked how and when it had gotten into me, the demon said it was when my uncle abused me sexually. It took advantage of the trauma to get inside me and make me hate men. It said it wanted to ruin my life, that it would never let me have a relationship with a man.

"The minister commanded it to come out of me and go away. The demon screamed that it would not leave, but the minister kept insisting, and I could feel it getting weaker. And then the demon started begging not to be expelled. It said it liked living in me. The minister just kept ordering it to leave, and suddenly I felt something like a gust of wind coming out of me. But something else took its place immediately, a force with a different personality.

"Suddenly I felt like a frightened child and I started shaking with fear. I could feel all this inside me, but I knew it wasn't me at all. I was experiencing the very feelings of the demon itself. This demon told about some very scary experiences I'd had. As it described each one, I would remember it and feel the same fear I had experienced at the time. The minister quoted a passage from the Bible, '... perfect love drives out fear' (1 Jn 4:18). When he said it, my body shuddered. Now I sensed that it was the demon that was scared at those words.

"The minister went on: 'Christ, the perfect love, casts you out. Fear, be gone in the name of Jesus.' My body shook violently, and tears rolled down my cheeks. I finally sensed that this demon had also left, and in my spirit I thanked God.

"There was another shift inside me, and a third demon came forward and identified itself as 'Hate.' It said its job was to instill me with hatred of other people, especially the people who had hurt me: hate the uncle who raped me, hate my parents because they didn't protect me, hate the teacher who spanked me at school, hate a high school teacher who wouldn't help me.

"At that point I felt like my whole body was oozing hatred, as if hatred itself had been personified in me and permeated me. The minister said, 'God doesn't want Eugenia to hate.'

"'Yes', replied the demon, 'but I force her to hate and she wants to hate.'

"'Why do you say that?' asked the minister.

"'She has not forgiven the people who hurt her, so I don't have to leave. I'm staying put!'

"Then the minister ordered the demon to give up control and let me speak. I instantly became myself again and I could talk.

"The minister asked me if I had heard what the demon was saying about my unforgiveness. I said I had, so he talked to me about the need to forgive every single person. He explained that my own failure to forgive was feeding that demon of hate and keeping it strong. He said I would need to forgive them all if I wanted this demon of hatred to leave.

"I told him if that's what it took to get rid of it, I was willing to forgive," said Eugenia, "but even so, I still felt angry and hurt every time I remembered those things. He assured me that God would take away these feelings if I obeyed his command to forgive. The minister guided me through a prayer of forgiveness, and I repeated it after him. When I did this, I felt peace and a sense of relief. Then the minister talked to the demon again and ordered it to leave because now its root had been cut off. It left immediately without even fighting back.

"Then the fourth demon spoke and said it was 'Guilt.' It said it made me feel dirty and guilty for what had been done to me. Guilt's job was to bring images into my mind to relive what had happened and make me feel bad again. It made me think that no man could ever want me after that. The minister quoted some Bible passages about God's forgiveness and about his promise to cleanse us. The demon cringed when it heard those words. It felt defeated.

"The minister said, 'You're defeated, Guilt. Admit it and get out. You can't stay here any longer.' Guilt said it didn't want to go. The minister kept ordering it to go, and it kept refusing. Even so, I could feel it getting weaker until finally it said, 'Fine! I'll go for now, but I'll be back!' But the minister said it was forbidden ever to return. Then he prayed, asking God to protect me, and as he did, I felt that alien force fading gradually away and started feeling like my normal self again.

"It was all so incredible!" marveled Eugenia. "Once it was over, I felt exhausted, but I started to cheer up. I've been feeling fine ever since. The strange sensations have left and there's nothing weird going on in my bedroom anymore. The nightmares haven't returned and everything seems to be all right."

I had listened attentively to the whole story, and it made a powerful impact on me. Something inside told me I had to find out more, so I asked Eugenia for the minister's phone number to call him. I decided then and there to look more closely into what this minister was doing and talk to other people who had had similar experiences with spiritual phenomena. I confess, though, that the whole thing filled me with indescribable fear.

CHAPTER 2

VÍCTOR MONTERROSO: THE DELIVERANCE MINISTER

I called the minister the very next day to ask about everything that had happened in Eugenia's session, and he spoke very openly. I drew up my courage and blurted out, "Could I watch you doing a case like this?"

He hesitated a moment, then replied, "It shouldn't be a problem. I'll set it up. Some of the people I am seeing would probably be willing if I explain that you are a Christian counselor and therapist."

I nearly leaped for joy, although deep down, I confess I was terrified. I had to wonder whether I was ready to see such things first-hand and whether they would affect me somehow. I had grown up in a Christian home, absorbing the stories told by visiting missionaries serving in Haiti, Brazil and Colombia. They talked about spiritual battles with demon possession, and their experiences sounded hair-raising! Although I wasn't sure I was ready to come face to face with such a case, I was determined to find out more, and I pressed on.

My professional training began to rear its head with a dizzying onslaught of questions. What if these cases are being mislabeled out of ignorance by people unversed in the sciences of psychotherapy? What if the phenomena actually have a scientific explanation and these pastors and ministers simply don't know enough? What if demons really can get into people and manipulate them however they want? What if I have a professional responsibility to investigate this, as both a psychologist and a Christian? What if I need to learn more about such phenomena before similar cases start coming into my office masked as mental illness? How can I tell the difference between a demon (if there is such a thing) and psychosis? What if they are the same thing? What does demonization even look like?

My mind reeled with it all. It was like an avalanche, and I couldn't hold it back. I felt as if I were opening a veritable Pandora's box, and hesitation and fear were fighting to hold me back. The minister agreed I could go to his church and watch next time he had a deliverance session. In the meantime, he suggested I stop by his office to pick up a recording from an earlier session so I could learn more about the process. He was extraordinarily candid with me.

That afternoon I went in to pick up the cassette and listened to it the same night. It was a two-hour recording. I sat through it twice, transfixed by everything I was hearing. As the so-called demon began to speak, I felt chills all over. I said to myself, "For the first time I am hearing the voice of a spirit. This is horrible! I didn't know you could hear them speaking!"

My scientific mind immediately leapt into the fray. "This is terrible! Someone has lured this poor woman into believing she is possessed, but the strange talk coming out of her mouth is just a symptom of her illness. She is hallucinating. She truly believes the devil is inside her, and she is acting out."

But I kept listening, more and more astounded by what the so-called demons were saying. Their words dripped with terrifying violence and hatred. It was especially strange to hear them talk about the woman as the owner of the body they inhabited. It was clearly not a case of hypnosis, because her unconscious mind would have spoken in the first person. Instead, they referred to themselves as "us" and to the woman as "her."

Could it have been a case of multiple personality disorder? It reminded me of *The Three Faces of Eve* or *Sybil*. Why did they call themselves spirits instead of introducing themselves as other personalities, each with its own name? Why did the voice insist, "We are a satanic legion" instead of saying "We are the personalities?" As I listened on, I only became more baffled. I could find no rational explanation for what I was hearing.

Then the so-called demon told its story. "Her grandmother used to put little seeds inside her blouse to protect her from evil, and that's where I got in. Adela was five years old. Crazy old lady hauled out her old superstitions to "protect" her granddaughter. Ha! It's just what God doesn't allow, so in I went. I like it here. I like making her suffer and I love tormenting her!"

"But your job is done," said the minister. "Christ has come to set her free. You must go."

"Nope, not leaving yet. I'll go when I'm good and ready, no matter what you say!" The voice was screaming now.

"You go when I tell you to because you are bound, hand and foot." The minister was unruffled. "I am the one who tells you what to do. I have the authority of Jesus Christ and you know you must obey," he asserted.

"I don't want to!"

"No one asked what you want. I COMMANDED you to go."

Its pride and insolence vanished, and it began to whimper, "Please don't make me leave. Where else can I go? Let me stay just a little longer. I hardly bother her."

"Get out, in Jesus' name."

I could hear loud sobbing. "I don't want to. Please!!! I don't want to go back to the abyss! It's dark. It's horrible! I don't want to go back there."

"You can cry all you want, but I don't feel one bit sorry for you, after all the damage you have done. I order you to go immediately," the minister insisted.

"No," the voice whined. "Look how late it is! Time to go home! Your family is waiting for you. You're getting so tired. So just leave me alone," it pleaded.

"Get out, in Jesus' name. You cannot make me budge, and here I will sit until you are gone. You don't fool me one bit."

"Oh, all right. I'll go, but I'm moving into Adela's husband. I can make him good and sick."

"No, I have not given you permission to do that. You are going straight into the Abyss, in Jesus' name."

"Ugh, you are making me crazy with that name! I'm leaving because I am sick of listening to you."

"Yes, go. Do it now."

I could hear Adela coming back to her senses at that point because the pastor was saying, "How do you feel, Adela?"

She replied, "Tired, but I feel pretty good. My mind is in a fog. Everything is spinning."

"Yes, that's normal," he explained.

"But I feel relieved, kind of lighter."

"Did you feel it leaving?" asked the minister.

"I felt a sudden pain in my chest and then it was gone. That's when I could talk again and open my eyes. Thank you, Lord. Thank you, Jesus!"

CHAPTER 3

DINORAH: CURSED BY HER IN-LAWS

S ome time later, a woman contacted me and asked, "Do you know anyone who is familiar with deliverance? I think that's what I need."

"Well yes, as it happens, I was just recently talking to a minister who led a girl I know through deliverance," I answered.

"Could you get me an appointment?" asked Dinorah.

"Of course! Let me talk to him, and we can go in together. I want to be there, if you don't mind."

"Oh yes," she exclaimed. "I would feel better with you there."

The next morning I called the minister and requested an appointment for Dinorah. He agreed to see her and to have me sit in on the session. Time slowed to a crawl after I hung up the telephone (phone?). The morning dragged on as I struggled to focus on what my other clients were saying. They deserved my full attention, but I could scarcely contain the riot of wild thoughts and feelings that crowded my mind as I antici-pated the upcoming deliverance session. At last I would see for myself what it was all about. I would be able to weigh it more objectively.

I showed up at the church on Tuesday at the appointed time and walked toward the minister's office. I knocked on the door, pushed it open and peeked inside. He was already talking with Dinorah and invited me in. I sat down and listened as he led her in Bible study. He asked Dinorah to read certain passages aloud and describe in her own words what they meant. She was clearly having a hard time understanding the text. She said she felt nervous, and her vision clouded as she tried to read.

I sat quietly in a corner while the pastor explained to Dinorah why Jesus had come into this world. He said it was not only to save us and forgive our sins, but also to give us power so we could defend ourselves from demons and the attacks of the enemy. She was visibly ill at ease and could scarcely concentrate. The minister pressed on with patience and understanding until she succeeded in comprehending the message.

"I don't know why I feel so frightened and can't seem to focus," Dinorah mused. I usually love to read the Bible, but now suddenly all I feel is aversion to it."

"Don't worry," the minister reassured her. "It's perfectly normal in these cases. That distaste you are feeling is not your own, but comes from the being that is inside you. Those spirits know what we are up to and they know when they are in trouble.

As they finished reading the Bible, the minister said, "It's time to start rebuking the spirits. We will stand up to those demons and command them to go. Make yourself comfortable and we can begin.

"Heavenly Father, please set Dinorah free from the evil spirits that are tormenting her, and I ask it in Jesus' name. All spirits hiding in this woman, I am talking to you now in Jesus' name. I command you to speak. I want to talk to you."

Dinorah had closed her eyes and seemed to be praying, but she abruptly started to look around and then spoke in a snarl, "What do you want from me? Leave me alone!"

My heart skipped a beat and a cold chill ran up my spine.

"Who are you?" demanded the minister.

"Myself. Who did you think?" it answered with a sneer.

"Tell me your name," the minister insisted.

"I am Nerves."

"What are you doing in her?"

"Look for yourself! I make her tremble. See what I mean?"

"Yes, but you yourself tremble at the mere mention of Jesus' name. Who is Jesus, Nerves?"

"I don't know him."

"Jesus is the Son of God, and you do know him."

"Yes, I get it."

"So why did you deny it?"

"I don't like to talk about him."

"Why did Jesus come, Nerves?"

"Just to annoy us, and now you're annoying me too."

"Why do you say 'us?' Who else is in there?"

"Ask them yourself. I'm only giving my own name."

"I command you in Jesus' name to tell me who the other demons are."

"Depression and Magda," said the voice coming from Dinorah.

The minister pressed on: "Who is Magda?"

"A witch who has her all bound up. She used sorcery to destroy her marriage."

"Did Magda send you?"

"Yes, and I like it here. I harass her all I want, but now I'm nearly finished. Look at the state she's in! Ugly, fat and stupid! I don't let her read. She thought she was so smart, she used to read a lot. But now every time she opens a book, I tangle up her mind and get her all confused. Her husband is already thinking of leaving her. I have it all set up, and this marriage is over."

"Who paid Magda to do this work?"

"Her mother-in-law and her sister-in-law. They never did want him to marry her."

"Nerves, I am aware that you know what the Bible says."

"You're right about that—better than you do!"

"So you know it says that *whatever we bind on earth will be bound in heaven, and whatever we loose on earth will be loosed in heaven* (Mt 16:19)."

"Shut up! I don't want to hear that!"

"You don't like to hear the Bible because it's God's Word and because it has power over you."

"I just don't like it; so what? I'm not listening any more." Dinorah's hands flew to cover her ears. "I won't listen. I can't hear you." It started singing with her hands over her ears.

The minister snapped, "Put those hands down!"

"I don't want to," it protested, but Dinorah's hands fell into her lap.

"I release Dinorah from the power of witchcraft, in Jesus' name."

"No, no!" the voice bellowed.

"And I bind you, Magda, and your spirit of witchcraft, and command you to come out of her, in the name of Jesus."

Dinorah's face turned toward the corner where I was sitting, and she thrust a finger toward me.

Ashen, terrified and panic-stricken, I fought the urge to flee. "O my Lord," cried my spirit, "Protect me! Why did I ever come here? I'm not ready to watch this. I'm afraid!"

"No!" I could hear the minister speaking in a level voice. "She is a child of God and you cannot enter her."

I was startled at his calm demeanor, as it seemed that he was not the least bit affected by it all. "How can anyone ever get used to this?" I wondered in horror.

"Go now to the Abyss," he continued.

"No! Not there!" wailed the voice.

"Into the Abyss this minute, in Jesus' name."

Dinorah yawned loudly several times, and the minister urged her on, "Yes, that's the way. Out of her completely. To the Abyss, in Jesus' name. Thank you, Lord. You are setting Dinorah free."

After a few moments of calm, Dinorah's body began to shake uncontrollably as tears rolled down her cheeks and she shook with sobs. "No, no! I'm so frightened!"

"Who are you?" the minister demanded again.

"Fear."

"How long have you been there?"

"Twenty years."

"How did you get in?"

"A dog bit her when she was three years old. She was very frightened and that's where I got in."

"Did you enter alone?" inquired the pastor.

"I came in with Nerves because we work together. I scare her all the time; I have lots of ways. I just love all her fears. They make me stronger and then Nerves causes her to tremble and gives her palpitations. He makes her dizzy and then I tell her she'd better not go outside. Now that really scares her! So she doesn't work any more and never goes anywhere."

"Who is Jesus, Fear?"

"You already know, so why ask me?"

"Who is stronger, you or Jesus?"

"He is, but I'm strong, too."

"Not anymore you aren't, because I am binding you in Jesus' name and taking away your power.

Can you feel the chains?"

"Damn you! You'll pay for this! Just wait until we meet again!"

"I break the power of your curse and cast you out in Jesus' name. Stop threatening me because there is nothing you can do."

"All right, I'm going. I've had it."

"Yes, go to the Abyss. You are defeated."

Dinorah heaved a loud sigh and suddenly stopped shaking. She looked at the minister and asked, "Is it over?"

"Yes, it's gone."

"This is all so strange!" she cried. "I could hear everything they said but it wasn't me! How can these things even exist? I'm here because a friend pushed me into coming, but I didn't really believe any of it. The only reason I went along with it was because I was desperate, but I never thought it was possible. How can a Christian have demons anyway? The Holy Spirit is supposed to be living in me and everyone always says demons can't be where the Holy Spirit is."

"Many people have asked me that very question," replied the minister. "In fact, I thought the same thing myself before I started seeing it all, and now I realize it is not correct doctrine. If they speak through your mouth and move your body, then somehow they are inside you. So of course you never seemed to get any better, even when you asked God to heal you. It was never an illness to begin with, but just those demons living inside you and manipulating you through your own mind. The demons leave when you cast them out in Jesus' name, which is why we need deliverance. You will never really have God's peace in your life until they are gone.

"Remember, the Bible describes Satan as the thief that comes to steal and kill and destroy. But Jesus said, '*I have come that they may have life, and have it to the full*' (Jn 10:10). Christians who cannot seem to win the victory over their problems will never have life to the full because something or someone is stealing it, and all too often, that someone or something is a demon. No wonder the Bible says, '*Resist the Devil, and he will flee from you*' (Jas 4:7). If you want Satan and the demons to leave you alone, you need to resist them in Jesus' name. Ignoring them will never make them leave. In fact if you ignore them, they are free to do whatever they want."

"No one ever explained this to me, even though I have known the Lord for years. Why don't they teach such things in the church?"

"Here, in this church, we certainly do teach it. Some churches have indeed distorted the doctrine of demons and Satan and even totally dismissed it. Nowadays hardly anyone believes that the devil and unclean spirits even exist, and that goes for Protestants and Catholics alike. Believe me, the devil has a much easier time of it when people think he doesn't exist. That way he passes unnoticed and no one stands up to him.

"Another common notion that works very well for Satan is that we need to be afraid of him. It is absolutely not true. The Bible is very clear about it: the one who is in you, that is God, is greater than the devil, who is in the world (1 Jn 4:4). We have power over him if we believe in God. In fact, the devil is the one who fears us and obeys us if we stand up to him in Jesus' name.

"Some people prefer to think that if they stay out of the devil's way, he will stay out of theirs. It's another lie. The devil wants to destroy everything God loves. In fact, he would rather destroy Christians than unbelievers because they are a threat to him. It's his way of getting even with God since Christians belong to God."

The conversation ended and it was late, so Dinorah said good-bye and left for home. It was to be a sleepless night for me. The experience shook me to the core and my mind could not rest. I spent many days trying to make sense out of everything I had seen and heard.

CHAPTER 4

RITA: YOUR TURN NOW!

I had sat transfixed through the whole session, fascinated and frightened, and after it was over, the minister did me a kindness that seemed at the time like a bad joke. The patient had left at the end of her deliverance session, and he turned to me and casually said, "Very well, Rita. Now you know how it's done. You are a Christian, and as a child of God, you have the same authority to cast out demons. The Bible says very clearly that whoever believes will be able to drive out demons in Jesus' name (Mk 16:17), so now it's your turn, and you know what to do. If you come across a case like this, you can handle it on your own."

I stared at him, bewildered. At first I thought he was kidding, but his face was telling me otherwise, and my heart sank. He was serious! I remained silent because I could not think of a thing to say. I felt like I was being torn apart. He was saying something I had never expected to hear, and he seemed blissfully unaware that I was still deeply shaken by what I had just seen. Or perhaps he could read it in my face and spoke out for that very reason. Regardless of what he was thinking, I have to believe that he spoke by divine inspiration, because his words instilled in me the courage I needed to undertake my personal journey into this mysterious spiritual realm.

I began to haunt Christian bookstores in search of material on demonology and satanism. I devoured them in my free time and sometimes late into the night. I had become desperately hungry to find out about *the works of the devil* that Christ had come to destroy (1 Jn 3:8). I thought about all my years growing up under Christian teaching and wondered why no one had ever taught me about these things. I was only now, at age 20, discovering that theological teaching about demons was nowhere to be found. Satan must have been very pleased with this state of affairs, but I decided to dive in headfirst and make up for lost time.

Around then I had been in close contact with another Christian counselor, and I asked him if he knew anything about this field. He told me about an urgent call he had once received to go immediately to a house where a young girl was deeply disturbed.

"I walked into the house," he explained, "saw the state she was in, and started to rebuke it 'just in case,' but nothing happened."

I found his words both astonishing and distasteful.

"How can a professional therapist start rebuking 'just in case?'" I wondered. "What if the person is not demon-possessed at all, but mentally ill? Wouldn't it be dangerous to throw this rebuking around so lightly? What about the power of suggestion? Couldn't he induce the patient to believe she is being controlled by a demon? Wouldn't this make her worse?"

No, I couldn't swallow it. "There has to be a better way," I thought.

Perhaps there was a more responsible approach, more systematic or even scientific, although the word "scientific" did ring a bit hollow in this context. I had never read any scientific research on such a subject.

"There must be a method, something more reliable, even measurable," I thought. I vowed not to rest until I had found it.

CHAPTER 5

GOD STEPS IN

God was not gentle with me. He threw me into the fray long before I felt ready. I had mapped out my whole program of preliminary research, but he had other plans altogether.

Even so, I trusted in his wisdom to do things his way. He certainly knew me, what a coward I was and how risk averse. I rarely ever took a step forward until I knew how it would work out. He knew that if he left it up to me, nothing would happen, so I needed a strong nudge. Of course I was not all pleased about it at the time, and I told him so in no uncertain terms; but he did what he had to do.

One night I was wrapping up a counseling session with a Christian client. My custom with believing clients was to close in prayer, surrendering the therapy to God and asking him to carry it through to completion. On an impulse I took her hand as I prayed. I had sensed she needed a human touch to support her at that moment.

No sooner had I begun to pray and intercede before God, asking him to help her overcome the fear and anxiety that troubled her, than the woman broke in and interrupted. "How strange," I thought, as I fully realized what she was saying:

"SHE BELONGS TO ME, AND I AM NOT LEAVING. STOP BOTHERING ME. LEAVE ME ALONE BECAUSE I LIKE LIVING HERE. YOU ARE SO ANNOYING!"

A shiver ran up and down my spine. I stiffened and opened my eyes. She looked like she was still praying, but the voice coming out of her mouth was taunting me. I realized I was still holding her hand and I didn't know what to do. My first impulse was to drop her hand and fling it away, but something inside me made me stop.

"If you do that," an inner voice cautioned, "the demon will know you are afraid of it and you will lose your advantage."

"But if I don't," I answered back, "I will drop dead of fright right here. I feel like I am holding the devil's own claw in my very hand! What if it comes into me through this physical contact? "

"Get hold of yourself," said the inner voice. "Remember what the minister said. You have God's authority, now use it!"

"Oh my God, " I cried out as I recognized the voice inside me. "Don't leave me now. I need you here beside me, so give me strength."

The woman's husband, also in the room, looked baffled.

Her mouth kept talking, but now I understood that it was a demon. It was a good first step, right? At least I had figured that out.

"SHUT UP, SHUT UP!" it said. "Stop praying for her. I am not going anywhere, and I refuse to let you ruin this."

I mustered up all the courage I could find—which wasn't much—and leaped into action. "What's your name?" I demanded.

"Nerves. I am Nerves, and I'm not alone. We have a whole crowd here and we are strong."

"How did you get in, Nerves?"

"I live here. This is my house."

"Answer me! How did you get in?" I snapped.

"Ah, there were so many things. She is very weak, so it was simple."

"What do you want with her?"

"We want to destroy her. We want her husband to get sick of her and walk out."

I didn't dare look away to glance at her husband. I was terrified that this woman might lunge at me, though she showed no signs of doing so.

"You will fail," I answered. "Come out of her in the name of Jesus."

"No, I am not leaving. I'm strong."

"Stronger than I am, for sure," I thought to myself, but I pressed on. "Stronger is he who is in me," I declared.

"Ah yes, but I am also strong. We will see who wins this," he dared me.

My mind was racing. It was ten o'clock at night, my husband was about to pick me up and there was no one else in the building to open the door for him. "It's closing time," I told myself. "What can I do?"

A thought came to me and I acted on it. "It's time to give back her control over her mind so she can go home," I ordered, trying not to show that I was trembling with fear.

The woman opened her eyes and said, "What happened?" She looked as if she were just waking up from a deep sleep.

I didn't know what to say. I looked at her husband and asked him, "Do you realize what happened?"

"I don't know what to think," he said. "I heard it all but I don't know what it was all about."

"I need to go now. It's very late, and I think we should talk about this at our next session," I said, warding off any lengthy explanations that I did not feel ready to give. They agreed and left. At first I felt relieved, but then I thought, "What if one of those spirits came out and is floating around here somewhere?"

The thought made me shiver. I took the Bible off the shelf and clutched it tightly against my chest with both hands. I tried to feel God's presence. "Lord," I begged, "please get my husband here on time!"

I inched through the hallway to the building's front door and cautiously pushed it open. Nothing! He wasn't there yet. I hugged my Bible all the way back to my office. "Oh, Lord! Please tell me there are no evil spirits around here, tell me that nothing will hurt me or get inside me."

I felt truly terrified. Then I heard the horn honking and knew he had come. I dashed to the door, walked out of the building and plunged into the car, still clinging to my Bible. "Thank you, Lord! Thank you for bringing him just in time!"

CHAPTER 6

A MINISTRY IS BORN

I attempted on numerous occasions to talk more with the minister who had started me off by letting me observe his own deliverance work, but he was overwhelmed with appointments at the time. I later discovered that this was par for the course for anyone willing to work in spiritual deliverance.

It was no use, and I finally gave up trying to call. His workload was so heavy that it was out of the question, so I had no choice—I needed to find other resources. I wanted to learn first-hand how other people handled these cases.

I was surprised to learn that a friend from my Bible study group had been through deliverance herself. She told me a powerful story about a prayer group that had helped her, added that she was still going back to the group occasionally and offered to take me along. I went several times until something happened that scared me away.

I had received a new client whose mental health condition was very fragile and who described a number of supernatural experiences she had been through. Her story was convincing, and I knew she needed deliverance. I tried again to contact the minister who had helped me, but I failed to reach him. Because the case was so urgent, I turned to this group even knowing it might be risky.

I asked a woman from the group to join me on a home visit to the patient, who at this point was bedridden and unable to get up. The plan was simply, to pay her a visit, pray with her and invite her to attend the group as soon as she was able, so we could minister inner healing and deliverance.

Her sister had agreed to take us to the house, but we got off to a bad start when she arrived very late. I had understood that she was going to drive us there, but it turned out we would be taking a bus. She showed up so late that it was already time for me to go home before we even left. I hated for her to waste her trip, to I asked the woman who had joined me from the prayer group to go without me, engage my client in conversation and invite her to a prayer meeting. She agreed and off they went.

The next day when I called my client to find out how she was and ask about the visit, I received a most unpleasant surprise. My client's mother answered the phone and told me that the woman's visit had been simply dreadful. Rather than just inviting my client to the prayer meeting, she had taken liberties, acted unbidden, and brought on a serious crisis.

The woman from the group was a charismatic Roman Catholic, and I had explained to her that the family she would be visiting was Protestant. I had asked her please to stay away from any controversial topics, but she had ignored my request and seized the opportunity to gain a convert to Catholicism. I had made a terrible mistake!

She had also confronted the demons that were tormenting my client, without any prior explanation. When they manifested violently, she screamed at them and ordered them out. The family members were horrified. When my client begged for them to get this person out of the house, the woman just pressed on fighting demons. Finally someone told her she had to leave.

The household was in complete pandemonium at that point. My client had sat through violent manifestations of multiple demons and was terribly upset. They decided to find a pastor to calm her down. She was thoroughly traumatized by the entire experience and furiously blamed me for it. She wanted nothing more to do with me, and I did not blame her. I had never intended for it to end this way, and the woman's unsolicited actions had gone far overboard and the harm she had done was incalculable. I was devastated. I had never lost a client under such unpleasant circumstances.

I went to talk to the Catholic woman from the prayer group and asked her to explain herself, but she refused to accept any wrongdoing. The last straw was when she told me the following story: "I remember one time when we were praying for a man. We rebuked the demons in Jesus' name but nothing happened. So one of the women in the group cried out, 'Demon, I cast you out in the name of Mary, Mother of God!' The man began to convulse and fell to the floor. All his symptoms vanished in an instant and he stood up. So you see? Mary has power too."

Her story shocked me. I knew the Bible well and I knew many passages by heart: *"For there is one God and one mediator between God and mankind, the man Christ Jesus"* (1Ti 2:5). *"And these signs will accompany those who believe: In my name they will drive out demons"* (Mk 16:17). I knew very well that deliverance was to be done through Jesus' name.

I quickly grew disillusioned with this group, and when I discussed it with my friend from Bible study, she too was shocked. "This confirms something God revealed to me while I was praying a few days ago," she said. "He told me that even though I had received deliverance in that group,

I should not return because they were moving down the wrong path. Now I see why."

I felt sad about the group and even sorrier for the many people who were going to them for help. All the people there had the best of intentions, but unfortunately their Biblical roots were not strong. It may have been wrong of me to walk away and never explain why I believed they were mistaken, but at the time I felt that I just needed to leave. I asked God to send his Spirit to guide them into the whole truth, as he promises in his Word.[1]

I stopped attending the group's meetings and continued to look for people experienced in ministering spiritual deliverance. I found a few, all of them overwhelmed with work and unable to meet with me.

"This cannot be a coincidence," I mused. "The demand for their services must be greater than I ever guessed." Clearly, it was a field that needed willing workers. So I finally understood that God was pushing me to start out on my own. I felt absolutely unprepared for such a step, and I discussed it very frankly with God.

"Lord, I feel like I am on very shaky ground," I objected. "I have far too little experience with

---

1 I want to clarify that casting out demons in Mary's name is not necessarily an accepted routine among charismatic Roman Catholics. I personally know many people who attend similar groups and who would never condone such practices. It was a single incident in one particular group, and I am not qualified to generalize any further.

these things. I have observed only a few sessions and I have never tried it on my own."

"Don't you remember what happened in your office the other night?" he whispered into my mind.

"Well yes, but that was different. You pushed me into it. But now you are telling me to call up these demons on my own."

"Do not let your heart be troubled and do not be afraid. I myself will help you. I will show you the way. I will be with you at all times. I will never leave you alone."

"Oh come on, Lord!" I moaned. "What you are asking is just too hard. I am a professional therapist and now my reputation is at stake. They will all think I have lost my mind. A clinical psychologist casting out demons! It's inconceivable! Besides, I don't even know how to do it."

"That's true," he replied. "Many will believe you have lost your mind. I already cautioned you about that in my Word: '*The person without the Spirit does not accept the things that come from the Spirit of God but considers them foolishness, and cannot understand them because they are discerned only through the Spirit*' (1 Co 2:14). Only trust in me. I am your guide."

"Lord, you know I'm not very strong, spiritually. What if a case turns violent and I can't handle it? What if I get hurt? What if Satan attacks my family? I have heard that Satan plays hardball with people who get into this business."

"I am your Protector, your Safe Refuge. I am your Strength."

"Lord, sometimes I don't quite trust your judgment. I really don't understand why you want someone like me for a job like this. You know how fearful I am. If you really mean to get me into this business, it will take far more than a just few tweaks. The whole building needs to be demolished and rebuilt from the ground up!"

"*For the Spirit God gave us does not make us timid, but gives us power, love and self-discipline* (2Ti 1:7). I built the universe. Do you doubt my ability to tweak your building a little?"

"Oh all right, Father. I accept. Send me all the cases you want. I'll do my best, but I can't promise anything."

"Slow down. The outcome is my doing, not yours. You will be nothing more than a channel of my power."

"You're right, Lord, forgive me."

Thus it was that a bad experience clinched it for me, and I decided to dive straight into the ministry of deliverance from demonic powers. I thank God for his promise: *"And we know that in all things God works for the good of those who love him, who have been called according to his purpose"* (Ro 8:28).

CHAPTER 7

MARUJA: PLAYED TOO PASSIVE A ROLE

I t was not long afterward that Maruja came to me for help. She had received deliverance from the same minister I knew, and although she was doing much better, she needed follow-up assistance, and he would not be available for another few months. A friend had given her my name, and she wondered whether I would be willing to continue with the work. Somehow I mustered the courage to take her on, and of course I know full well who gave me the confidence to proceed. My Lord was nudging me along, leading me with his love on the path he had marked out. It was an adventure into the unknown, and I have never regretted going off on this journey with him.

The most daunting challenge for me in the early days of the ministry was the anxious uncertainty of not knowing whether the demons would manifest. Maruja had already begun her work with the pastor, and the demons had manifested openly in her sessions with him, so at least in this case I knew where we stood and felt less anxious.

We started with prayer, and I began to confront the spirits. They responded almost immediately, and the battle was on. As the session unfolded, I began to see clearly that the power of God was indeed working within me as the spirits followed my orders to speak out and answer my questions. I began to feel a courage that was new to me.

Even so, I admit that I was frightened by some of the things they said. One of them snickered, "Fine! I will come out of her and move right into you."

My heart did a backflip, and although somewhere deep inside I knew it was impossible, I felt like I was being pushed toward doubt.

"You can't do that," I pointed out timidly. "Christ is protecting me."

"Ha, ha," it cackled. "But I scared you, didn't I?"

Such episodes, I found, did not last long and tended to make me stronger in the Lord.

My work with this client continued for quite some time. She had clearly improved, but eventually we seemed to reach an impasse because she was not doing her part. She found it easy to come into my office, take her seat and just let me wage the spiritual battle for her, while she did nothing to help.

I became utterly frustrated in one session when I began to encounter the very same spirits we had cast out the last time. I asked what they were doing there, and they replied, "She does not draw on God's strength and power. She is so weak that we can come and go whenever we please."

This set me to thinking. I realized that the battle with demons had to take place alongside a process of spiritual growth through Bible study and involvement in spiritual groups. Not only that, I also understood that the battle should unfold hand-in-hand with a process of psychological maturing and life-style changes. Otherwise, the results could never last.

She was working with two other counselors at the same time, figuring this would speed things up a little. The result was utter confusion, as none of us knew what was happening in the sessions with the others. I finally confronted her about it and told her she needed to pick one of us to be her regular deliverance counselor, pointing to the drawbacks of continuing as she was. I also explained that she needed to take a more active role in her own treatment and start helping herself along, including both spiritual work and practical actions. For example, she needed to start spending her days in useful pursuits, as she had very little to occupy her time.

As it happened, one of the other ministers counseling her made the very same sugges-tion, and she had to believe we were right. She began to take more responsibility for her own life instead of drawing stability entirely from others. Her progress picked up speed as she organized her life better.

Her case taught me that deliverance in and of itself was not enough. Lasting results required a combination of spiritual growth, psychological skills and practical life decisions.

CHAPTER 8

ALEJANDRO: OBSESSIVE-COMPULSIVE DISORDER

Alejandro was a forty-year-old bachelor I had been treating for about a year. He was suffering from a condition known in psychology as "obsessive-compulsive disorder."[2] His particular obsessive compulsion involved cleanliness.

Although he lived several hours away and had to commute to my office, I was impressed that he made the effort to drive so far just to attend his appointments. I could see how much he wished to be better and to invest whatever effort was necessary to gain emotional health.

---

2   OBSESSIVE-COMPULSIVE DISORDER: A persistent, uncontrollable conviction that the conscious mind cannot ignore and that drives sufferers to perform certain acts against their own will and contrary to their sense of what is rational.

He lived with his parents and brother, and his symptoms caused them endless problems. He was tormented by the perception that his family was too careless about personal hygiene, and day after day he harangued them to wash their hands, especially after going to the bathroom. They tried to be understanding, but he nagged them so incessantly that they often lost patience and got into shouting matches with him.

Alejandro was obsessed with avoiding contamination. If he needed to open the door, he would wrap a clean handkerchief around the doorknob to protect his hand from touching it directly because he was terrified that germs might be on it. He even had to wash coins to make them safe. He showered several times a day, lathering up repeatedly. Afterward he worried that he had missed some part of his body. He never felt truly clean.

He refused to eat at restaurants or in other homes for fear the people cooking were not clean enough. He gagged at the very thought. In his own home, he would not sit down to eat without first washing his own dishes and silverware. He pestered his mother incessantly, asking if she had washed her hands before touching the food.

Toilets were desperately revolting to him. He was always equipped with plastic bags just in case he needed to defecate, because he was horrified at the idea of sitting on a toilet seat that had been used by someone else. He had his own private bathroom in the home and kept it impeccably clean.

The science of psychology has found that cleanliness compulsions originate with unconscious feelings of guilt that make sufferers feel dirty. They mask this unconscious condition by projecting their sense of guilt/uncleanness onto others and convincing themselves that everyone else is dirty.

He was a Christian but had become inactive. Our conversations led him to rejoin the church, which had helped assuage his feelings of guilt, but many of his symptoms persisted nonetheless.

I was praying with him in a session one day when I felt the urge to speak out. I declared in a clear voice, "In Jesus' name I break this obsession and order forgotten memories to surface into his conscious mind."

He reacted at once and began to weep bitterly. "I am seeing memories," he sobbed. "I had completely forgotten about them. I was lying in bed one day when I was very young, and my mother suddenly yanked away the blankets and caught me touching my penis. She bawled me out and said I should never do such a filthy thing. I was ashamed, and I cried and cried.

"I am also remembering that I used to take care of some of the neighbor girls who were younger than I was. I didn't like one of them, so I would hit her all I could whenever the adults weren't around. She was smaller than I was and couldn't defend herself, and I would threaten her and warn her not to tell anyone. I knew it was wrong, but I just couldn't stop myself.

"There was something else my mother would do. If she thought I had touched something dirty, she would slap my hand and say 'poopy!' Maybe that's one of the reasons I find toilets so disgusting."

So I prayed and asked God to heal his wounds and take away the lingering sense of guilt from these incidents. I also asked God to heal the strong association between "poopy" and "dirty." Only then did I proceed to minister deliverance.

My client felt great relief after this experience. He stopped pressuring his family so much and found himself lathering only once when he bathed.

This case showed me that a demon's power over a person is very closely interwoven with his or her psychological traumas. He or she needs to unearth memories that hold a destructive emotional charge because experiences in the past can gradually morph into a psychological condition. Only after the individual understands this and asks God to heal the emotional wounds can we proceed to cast out any demon that may have entered as a result of the trauma. I have observed, however, that if the trauma remains hidden below the surface of the conscious mind, the demon will refuse to leave because the trauma provides it a permanent foothold. The evil spirit is solidly attached to this forgotten memory.

I realize that the Bible does not discuss any of this. It does narrate several cases that are resolved simply by ordering the demon to leave, and out it goes. So why is it so different today? Although I wish I had the full answer, I can at least offer a few thoughts on the subject.

In Biblical times, the sciences of the mind and emotions were unknown and human behavior was a mystery. Today we know a great deal more, and we can use this knowledge as never before. I believe God works with each of us according to our own individual degree of knowledge. This is why the book of James says, "Not many of you should become teachers, my fellow believers, because you know that we who teach will be judged more strictly" (Jas 3:1). If God has given us greater knowledge, he also expects more from us.

He gave me the opportunity to study psychology, and he expects me to use what I have learned. It would be so much easier for me if I could perform deliverances like the ones in the

Bible: "Out in Jesus' name," and the demon goes. If it were that simple, though, neither my client nor I could ever figure out how the demons got in. Nor could we guess what measures are needed to keep the demons away or even prevent them from attacking subsequent generations.

I was able to help this obsessive-compulsive patient understand that his mother had been deeply wrong when she shamed her four-year-old son for touching his penis and when she programmed him to be revolted by his own feces. If he had not gained this understanding, he would most likely have done the same thing some day to his own future children. Why is this? We all tend to replicate with our own children the same mistakes our parents made with us, unless something intervenes to correct our mistaken ways of thinking.

These demons of guilt and revulsion did not leave when I first ordered them out, so I had to probe more deeply in order to pinpoint his mother's mistakes. Now, thanks to developments in the science of psychology and to his own discoveries about his past, he was able to understand that touching his penis at the age of four was not a sin, but completely normal behavior for a young boy discovering his own body. He also learned that children should not be taught to associate the notion of "poopy" with "dirty," as his mother did.

CHAPTER 9

CECILIA: A NINE-YEAR-OLD CHILD

"Please help my child," begged Cecilia's mother. "We are not part of the national health service, and I can't afford a therapist. Her teacher says she needs professional help because she's having so many problems at school."

I set an appointment, and when the day came, she arrived with the child. Cecilia was nine years old. I spoke with her alone, and she told me she could hardly concentrate in class or pay attention to the teacher. She was having trouble learning, and this was why they had come to my office.

Counselors understand, though, that our clients' first explanations are not always the main problem. We have been trained to dig deeper and look beyond their opening remarks. I asked about her family. Cecilia's parents were separated and her alcoholic father was very violent. She had often seen him beating her mother. I asked how she felt about her mother, and she told me she loved her and they got along well.

"Your mother tells me that sometimes you say very unkind things to her." I asked, "Are you angry with her about something? Do you wish she lived with your father?"

Cecilia began to cry. "I love my father. I know he is bad to Mama and so we can't live with him. But I understand that, and it's not the reason why I say mean things to Mama. I don't know why I do it. I don't even want to," she added, sobbing.

"I wish you knew how I feel; sometimes it's like the devil gets into me and makes me say things. He forces me to tell my mom things like, 'Filthy bitch. Why did I have to be born to you? I would rather have been born to a dog.' I don't want to say it, but that voice forces me. It won't leave me alone until I do it. I know it's wrong, but I just say it anyway and then I start crying because Mama looks so sad."

I continued to probe, and she told me that a few years earlier, she used to have a friend no one else could see. Her mother couldn't see him, and nobody could except her. His name was Juan, and they would spend hours talking and playing together.

Then she said, "Juan doesn't come to play with me any more, but my dead Granny does. She comes and sings to me, always the same song, and she talks to me and then she vanishes. My little sister Elisa sees her too. Elisa always goes around singing that same song of Granny's."

All these things together suggested that the child might be under the influence of demons. I asked her to wait outside so I could speak with her mother. I wanted to discuss the matter further and ask permission to minister deliverance to Cecilia.

I told her my suspicion of what might be happening with the child, and her mother responded very candidly, "Now that you brought it up, there's something I should probably tell you. My parents were spiritists. They are no longer alive, but the girls tell me that Granny appears to them, and I know this can't be good.

"Strange things have happened to me, too. I was home alone one night when someone pounded on the door, and I answered. No one was there, but something came in and pressed me against the wall and then threw me to the floor. I nearly died of fright and I just lay there on the floor crying in terror. I haven't told anyone because they would think I was crazy."

I offered a brief explanation about demons and how to confront them. I then asked permission to pray for her daughter, and she readily agreed. "I don't know anything about these things," she cautioned, "but everyone recommended you, so I trust you."

The mother left and Cecilia came back into my office. I explained my thoughts in the simplest terms. I told her that the voice she was hearing, the one that ordered her to insult her mother, might not be coming from her own mind, but from something else that wanted to trouble her. I told her we were going to find out whether I was right.

I also stressed that God had power over anything that tried to hurt her and that if she wanted God's protection, it was very important to ask Jesus to come into her life and live in her heart. He would always be able to help from inside her.

"Cecilia", I added, "the Bible says that Jesus is standing at the door of your heart, knocking for you to let him in."

She answered unhesitatingly, "I can hear him! He's knocking on the door and I hear him right now!"

I was astonished. "Either this child has a fantastic imagination," I thought, "or God is really doing something inside her." I spoke to him in my spirit. "You know, God, I don't much understand what you are doing, but to her it seems like the most natural thing in the world to be feeling what you are showing her. Thank you for this help."

"Can you still hear him?" I asked.

"Yes," Cecilia replied, "he's still there!"

"Do you want to open the door of your heart to let him in?"

"Yes, I do!" replied Cecilia.

"Then tell him so."

"Jesus, come on in. I want you to come into my heart ... There, he did it," she cried. "He says H

he came in."

"Is he speaking to your mind?" I asked in wonder.

"Yes, I can hear him."

"Very good," I encouraged her. "Now I want to talk to the voice that has been bothering you and find out its name. If you hear the answer in your mind, just tell me. Will that work?

"Yes."

"In Jesus' name I bind everything that does not come from God. I call to whatever is in Cecilia and command you to tell me your name."

"They said there are three of them," Cecilia explained. "One is Juan, my friend when I was little, and the others are Ramón and Álvaro."

"Where have you settled in her?" I asked.

Cecilia touched her head and said, "Right here. They say in my head."

"Very good," I said, still startled that the child seemed so natural with all this and that she heard the spirits' voices so clearly. "Do you remember who just came into your heart?"

"Jesus. Juan says he sees Jesus in my heart. He's angry and says why did I let him in."

"Juan was pretending to be your friend," I explained, "but all he really wanted was to hurt you. Now you have a true friend, Jesus, and you can ask him to get rid of Juan and the other two. Jesus is stronger than they are."

"Jesus," said Cecilia, "please take away Juan and Ramón and Álvaro so they will stop bothering me and talking in my head. All done! They left because Jesus took them away!" Cecilia cried excitedly.

"Thank you, Jesus," I prayed. "Please do not let them come back. You stay with her and take care of her always."

"Cecilia, there is something I want to explain. The woman you see, who says she is your Granny, is not telling the truth. That's a lie. It's a spirit that pretends to be Granny to confuse you. Your Granny is dead, and the Bible says that after people die, we cannot talk to them any more because their spirit goes to another place and cannot come back to our world. If that spirit says it's Granny, you just tell it, "You are not my Granny. Don't come talk to me any more. I order it in Jesus' name."

The next week, Cecilia's mother told me that they had been in town the very evening following our session and had walked past a Christian church. Her daughter wanted to go inside. She insisted, "I'm a Christian and this is where I want to go. I need to learn about God."

My heart gave a lurch as I recognized God's hand in this child's life. He was taking things much further than I had intended. I had not told her to go to church, nor had I even used the word "Christian," which people in Costa Rica often misunderstand to mean "Protestant." I was being careful to respect her mother, a Roman Catholic. It was clear, though, that Cecilia had a special gift of clearly hearing God's voice and that he was leading her from within.

"Hallelujah!" rejoiced my spirit. "Lord," I murmured, "your deeds are truly great and wonderful."

Cecilia's mother told me they had entered the church, but that something awful had happened once they were inside. She herself had begun acting out, as if she were mentally disturbed. As she felt an uncontrollable rage washing over her, she began picking up the heavy church pews and flinging them around the room. A group of people gathered around her in a circle to pray. She began tearing off her clothes and screaming. It took eight persons to hold her down as they rebuked the demons inside her until at last she calmed down.

"They told me the spirits had left, but I don't really believe they are gone because I'm still feeling strange things," she told me.

"Would you like me to lead you in deliverance?" I asked.

"I do want that, yes, but I'm afraid. Here you are, all by yourself, but it took eight people to hold me down at the church. What if I get out of control again?"

"Don't worry about that," I replied. "It happened that way because you were in a church, and demons like to interrupt worship service to show off how strong they are and scare everyone. Instead of people all coming around you in a circle to rebuke it, they probably should have taken you into a side room and commanded the demons to quiet down and stop the violence; this would likely have put a stop to it."

"Well I guess so," she said, "if you say so. I just want to get rid of anything evil inside me."

I started by asking God to protect us and ordered the spirits to reveal themselves calmly, quietly and in order. So they began to speak but refrained from altering her behavior in any way.

They were all still there, even though they had fooled the people at the church into believing they had gone. The only thing they had done was stop manifesting and simply go back into hiding so all the rebuking would stop.

The strongest spirit in her was Fear. It had taken a powerful hold on her as her husband's beatings gathered strength. I ordered it to go out in a yawn, a tactic that had worked for me in the past, but the spirit just kept manifesting.

After a while it said, "I can't leave like that."

"So how can you leave?" I asked.

"By crying out to God," it replied.

"Great," I answered. "Go ahead!"

"Jesus!" it cried in a loud voice.

The woman's entire body shook, and then just as suddenly, calm reigned again. I asked her if she believed the demon had left completely.

"Yes, now it is gone," she replied. "I felt it leaving and now I just feel peace."

This case as well as others showed me that demons do not all leave in the same way. Some can be yawned out, while others produce vomiting or hemorrhage. Some leave through coughing, sneezing, urinating, shivering, sweating or crying, while others may go out through the ears or even without any physical manifestation whatsoever.

CHAPTER 10

ANA: A SHADY DEAL

Ana first came to me when her son was seven and her daughter was three, and she was in her final year of college.

"All my life I have had serious problems," she sighed in discouragement. "My mother had the same issues and it made her miserable to see that I had inherited them all. She spared no effort and no expense to find a solution for me. She took me to doctors, priests and even witches to help me get better. Poor thing, none of it worked and it broke her heart. No one could help me, and she died knowing I was no better."

"I understand how she suffered because now I am going through the same thing she did. My son is starting to show all the same symptoms, so now I am not only lugging my own problems around, but I need to watch him suffering too. It's like a family curse, like something passed down from generation to generation.

"I don't even 't know where to begin," Ana moaned. "So many things have happened to me, and most people don't even believe it when I tell them. They think I'm crazy. Psychiatrists certainly can't figure it out. The last time I was hospitalized by the national health service, they shot me up with their strongest drugs, at the highest doses, and it wasn't even enough to put me to sleep.

"They took me into a meeting room to talk with a medical board. They were asking me all kinds of questions, and after a while I just started making fun of them. It wasn't really me, though, I know that. It was something inside me, but not part of me. I don't really know how to explain it. It was someone who talked to the doctors using their own technical words, making fun of their diagnosis. It said words I don't even know. I was more surprised than they were to hear what was coming out of my mouth!

"The doctors were stunned to see such a change come over me, and they said it was a case of dissociative identity disorder, or multiple personalities. They wanted to keep me in the hospital awhile to study my case, but I asked my husband to take me home. The doctors said my treatment would take a long time and that the hospital was not really equipped for it, so they suggested we look into private medicine to get treatment but warned it would be very expensive. We didn't have the money, so I didn't even bother to ask for recommendations.

"I hear voices. I see things. I feel strange sensations. Sometimes I even have special powers. I feel myself being taken out of my own body, but I don't want that. I plead with God all the time to set me free of this condition and lead me to someone who can really help me. My son's teacher gave me your name and here I am to see what you can do.

"I have a friend at work who's a parapsychologist, and when I told him about my symptoms, he offered to help. I started going to him, but after awhile I realized he was practicing witchcraft, and I decided not to go back. At least I know enough to distinguish one from the other and to know what truly comes from God. I know God condemns spiritism, and I don't want anything to do with it. He pressured me a lot, trying to convince me. He told me I had special powers and I had no right to be selfish. He said I should use my powers to help people and he could train me, but I refused. He's still nagging me about it. He even comes to bother me in my dreams, but I won't have it."

"What do the voices tell you?" I asked.

"Mainly they want me to start a cult, a false cult, of course. They want to use my powers to confuse people and lead them away from the truth. I cry out to God and ask him to protect me. I absolutely will not do it because I love God.

"Now they're after my son, using him to pressure me. They harass him and frighten him so much that he can't even concentrate on his studies. That's how they want to break me because they say if I don't go along with them, they will hurt him."

"Who wants you to start this cult? 'They' who?"

"It's a group of spiritual masters, or anyhow, that's what they call themselves. I can see them, all dressed in white, standing in a circle and calling me to join in. But I refuse and cry out to God, which makes them furious.

"They try to tempt me by describing all the plans they have for me. They say if I go alone into the mountains, put on a white robe and meditate, they will come and start training me. They say they will teach me everything I have to do. They try to convince me by offering things they know I want or need.

"Someone took me to a Christian minister, and even though he helped me a lot and I'm doing much better, I stopped going. Lately I've been going to a Pentecostal pastor, who has also helped me a lot. He prayed for my son and me, and even though I'm very grateful for all his help, I don't like going to his church. The services are far too noisy for me and I need to find another place."

I responded by inviting her to visit my own church. I explained it was a Christian congregation, and the members were knowledgeable about evil spirits and how to fight them. I told her they also knew about spiritual gifts such as her own, including the gifts of vision and revelation, and that worship was not noisy, but very moving. She appeared interested and said she would go.

A week later Ana was back in my office. "Last Sunday," she said, "something very strange happened. I was getting ready to go to your church, and just as I stood up to go, my body went rigid. I was completely paralyzed, I couldn't move. My husband tried to get me back into the chair, but it was impossible because I was so rigid. I asked him to get me onto the floor, and I lay there for the whole three hours I would have been at your church.

"While I was there on the floor, I fought back the way you taught me, in Jesus' name. I used the Bible passages you showed me and commanded the spirits to leave. My husband wanted to take me to the hospital, but I didn't let him and told him Jesus would get me out of this. After a while I began to feel better and could move again. Little by little I recovered mobility, but it was not enough, and I had to miss work for two days."

I spent the rest of our appointment teaching her more about using the power of Jesus to fight off the spirits. The whole time we were talking about it, her body shook uncontrollably and she had trouble focusing her eyes enough to read the Bible passages I was showing her. She felt dizzy and strange, but we pressed on with the Bible study. We read the text on spiritual warfare in Ephesians 6:10-18, and she understood it all. At last we were ready to begin the actual deliverance.

I asked God for extra special protection, as I was going to work alone. Then I said, "I bind all unclean spirits in this woman. Now show yourselves, and no acting up."

No sooner had I said these words, than her wrists slammed together as if something invisible had grabbed them. Then a spirit began to speak," I am Sarai. I am part of the group."

"Do you have a foothold in this woman?" I asked. "Do you draw strength from something inside her?"

"Oh yes," it replied. "It's her friend the parapsychologist. He uses her as a medium and she doesn't even realize it."

"In Jesus' name I break his power over her. I also sever all demonic ties in her family that have passed from generation to generation, from both father and mother."

"No!" shrieked Sarai in desperation. "Don't do that! After all our hard work, don't break our power. We have been at it for generations now, it has taken so very long!"

"Too late, Sarai," I answered. "I just did it. Your power is broken."

"But we have a leader," she whimpered back, "a very powerful one."

"Ah ha. So who is your leader?" I asked.

"Satan."

"Is he here now?"

A guttural voice growled back, "Of course I'm here. I'm their leader."

"Satan, I have bound your powers. I will allow no violent manifestations," I ordered.

I said it more to quell my own fear and boost my spirit, than to remind him of what he already knew. It was the first time since I had begun this ministry that I came up against Satan himself. My earlier battles had been against demons, but never against their very leader. I had often wondered whether I would be prepared to fight him, but now my time had come. God was bringing me face to face with Satan, and there was no one else there to help me.

"Satan," I said, "who has been messing with my tape recorder?"

A grotesque howl of laughter burst from Ana's lips. "This is far too important" he snarled, "and I am not going to let you tape it. We need to protect ourselves."

I had been wrestling with the tape recorder ever since the spirits had begun to talk, but it continued to malfunction. Ana had commented in our previous meeting that the Pentecostal pastor who had been ministering to her had tried on three different occasions to tape her sessions, but something always went wrong. Even so, I had not expected to have trouble recording, because I had always been able to tape my previous sessions. The tape recorder refused to budge.

About that time I remembered the fresh batteries I had stowed in my purse. I pulled them out and smugly installed them in the stubborn machine. "Simple," I thought. "Low batteries."

I tried again, but to no avail. I prayed silently, "Lord, I don't know what's wrong with this machine, but I want to tape the session. Please make it happen."

I examined the cassette itself and found that the tape had come to the end. I knew perfectly well that it was fully rewound and ready when I placed it in the slot with the right side up, because the other side already had another recording on it. How did they manage to fast-forward the tape all the way to the end without touching the recorder? I will never know, but the fact is that it happened; praise God I realized it in time to rewind the tape to the beginning.

I bound all spirits interfering with the recorder and had no further problems with it. "Satan" I declared in a loud voice, "you keep your hands off my tape recorder and I will tape this session, like it or not. That is an order, in Jesus' name."

"I hate you," he growled furiously. "I curse you a thousand times and I will destroy you."

"God's word says in Isaiah 44:25, '... *who foils the signs of false prophets and makes fools of diviners, who overthrows the learning of the wise and turns it into nonsense, ...*' I break the power of your curse against me, in Jesus' name. I am not afraid of you, Satan. God is here and he is protecting me."

"Release me!" shrieked the devil. "Power lies in her hands and I can show you my power. Go ahead, let's fight fair."

"I don't need you to show me your power, Satan. It's clear that I am the one who has power over you. All I said was 'I bind you in Jesus' name,' and if that's all it took to tie you up and strip away your power over me, I am not much impressed by your swagger."

"I, Satan, order all the powers and principalities of hell to overpower this wretched bitch and shut her up. Let me go! I command all of you now!"

"They can't, Satan," I told him. "They are all bound up, just like you."

"Damn you, you filthy degenerate!"

I burst into songs of worship to God, drowning out the insults he was hurling at me. I read Psalm 83 aloud, using it as a personal prayer, asking God to destroy my enemies. Satan was furious. He was desperately struggling to free Ana's hands, but they remained stubbornly stuck together at the wrists. He was cursing me and bellowing at the top of his lungs, when he abruptly decided to change his tactics.

"I can give you whatever you want: power, riches, anything, because I am king. Ask me for anything, and it's yours."

"Only God can give me the things I truly desire," I answered, "and besides, you are no king. Weren't you cast out of heaven for making just such a claim? Don't you remember? And now here you are again, cast out of this woman for the very same sin. You just never learn, do you? No, I serve the King of kings" I said, "the Lord of lords. Your deal does not appeal to me in the slightest because serving him is the best thing I can do."

"You witch! Idiot! Fool! Let me go so we can fight! Just let me have Ana and her son. I need them to advance my kingdom and you can't have them. They're mine!"

"Not any more, they aren't. They have both given their lives to Christ in my presence. Jesus paid the price for their salvation with his blood, and now they belong only to him."

"Noooo! Don't say that!"

"What, blood of Christ?"

"Yes! It's a river and it crushes me."

"There's power in that blood," I said.

"Why are you fighting against me?" Satan asked.

"God sent me and it is God I serve. I told you that two years ago when I declared war against you right out loud. Don't you remember?"

"No! And I won't go. Why does God even bring people like her into the world? Why does she get such powerful gifts? I want them for myself!"

"God gave them to her to glorify him and serve others," I told him.

"Maybe so, but I'll get them in the end and I will use them myself. I can make her start my cult."

"No, you will not," I retorted. "Ana will follow God and use her gifts against you."

"No, you can't do that to me because I need her! I don't get it. How can a mere human hold off so long? Even when God was not inside her, she resisted me. Why is she so strong?"

"Enough, Satan. Be still and come out of her," I commanded.

"I, Satan, now order all you principalities and authorities to go and search throughout the world. Look among all the babies being born today and find someone. I need a person to carry out my plan, a person who has gifts like hers."

"No, Satan," I interrupted, "you will not go looking for another victim. I hereby send you and all your demons to the Abyss and Jesus will decide what to do with you."

"No, not to those pits! I don't want to go there."

"Obey, Satan! I order you in Jesus' name."

"All right, I'll go; but I warn you, we'll meet again. Just you wait, you'll see and you'll be sorry."

"My eyes will see only what God wants me to see. I will not see you because I do not want to see you."

Ana's body began to shake violently, and I had to hold her up to keep her from falling.

"Don't touch me!" Satan shrieked. "Get your hands off me!"

"Go, Satan, and take all your demons with you. Holy Spirit," I prayed, "use my hands as instruments of your power. Come now upon Ana to set her free and release her gifts to serve only God. Take control of her mind, her body and her spirit. Compel Satan to come out of her, and you take the place he was holding."

Ana's body was wracked with the strain as she coughed up thick mucous. "Ugh," she moaned. "What an awful smell! I can't stand the stink of it. I see dead bodies and I feel sick."

"Wait, Rita, now they're leaving! They're leaving! I can see them fleeing. They are horrid creatures, and they're trying to escape. Thank God! They really are leaving." Her hands finally flew apart and she raised them to God in praise. "I can see Jesus," Ana said. "I feel something warm and soft and I see a lovely bright light. It's all around me and he is getting closer. He's holding a cup to my lips for me to drink, and now he's pouring it over my head. I can feel the liquid entering my body, and it's delicious! It's wonderful!"

"Yes, Lord," Ana went on, I will serve you alone. I don't understand all these things that are happening, but now I know that you are with me. I will do what you ask of me, anything at all. Praise God! Thank you, Jesus."

Ana opened her eyes. "They're gone," she said. "I'm so tired, but it's all over. The only thing is, I don't think I can go to work like this, I'm just too weak. I need to sleep and I'd better go home. Thank you!"

The battle had lasted only an hour, unquestionably the most intense sixty minutes of my life. As I rethought the deal the devil had offered me, I felt very honored.

"Jesus," I said, "it's the very same deal that Satan offered you. "He held out power and wealth and asked me to serve him. It's an honor to have gone through the same temptation as you. And you know what? I didn't feel even the slightest desire to accept what he was offering. It tells me you really do control my life. Thank you, Jesus! Glory to your name!"

CHAPTER 11

AN UNBELIEVING PSYCHOLOGIST TALKS TO A DEMON

One day I was discussing some of my experiences in demonology with a non-Christian psychologist. As the conversation drew to a close, I suggested, "If you ever get a chance to sit in on a deliverance session, you should do it."

"Invite me yourself," he suggested. "I would go."

"I'll do that," I said, "I'll call you as soon as I get a case for you to observe."

It happened a few months later, so I called him and invited him to see deliverance for himself. The next day he showed up at my office for the appointment. He watched the proceedings very closely. He later attended a second session with the same patient, and afterward he asked whether he could interview her himself. She and I both agreed, and he spent a good fifteen minutes asking her every imaginable question, to which she replied openly.

Something very interesting happened in the third session. The demon presented itself as usual, and I turned to my non-Christian colleague and asked whether he would like to talk to it. He was intrigued and quickly accepted. I first bound the demon to truth and then let my colleague talk with it. I taped the entire dialogue and have transcribed it as follows:

"Who are you?" asked the psychologist.

"What? In whose name do you ask?"

"In the name of science."

The demon laughed out loud. "We do not reveal ourselves through science, and you have no power over me."

"So how do I know you even exist? After all, if you do not exist, you cannot torment Inés."

"Ah, but I do exist. I am real, but in the spiritual realm, not the material world. Ask whatever you like."

"What about this spiritual realm? How do I know there even is such a thing?"

"Well here I am, and I have a name. I am called Torment. I entered through her mind to oppress her, and it serves her right, because she is a daughter of the one they call God. Those are the ones we live to torment. They are our target and we must not let them get away."

"But why would you want to torment her?"

"There are two sources of power. We, with our principalities and authorities, come from hell and can move into people. The other one is the power of good. What we want, what I myself want, is to destroy her and torment her, get her to stop praying and stop seeking God so she will fall away from him and be like everyone else."

"So what's in it for you?"

"Ah, then I can have some fun. I go to God and say, 'See? I got her, even though you thought she was your daughter. But she backed down ... so many of them back down and now say they don't believe. Ha! They gave up so fast, they didn't even try. But here I am, still at work, and they haven't been able to get rid of me."

"But why do you want to win?"

"It would be evil triumphing over good."

"Whatever for?"

The demon laughed again. "The world is full of evil, and good itself has become so insignificant that it can never beat us."

"No one wants evil."

"Ah, but they do indeed."

"What could I want from evil?"

"Who, you? What do I know? Evil is in you. It lives in you and it lives in people, just like I live here. But I am Torment. I torment with evil, with destruction, with all that is ugly, all that is rotten, simply for the sake destroying, to break things apart. Evil is within you, deeply rooted, but she is different. I am in her mind, not inside her self.

"The being in me, is it the same one that's in her?"

"No, we have a group here working on her, but the ones inside you are different. You have so very many."

"Can you see the beings inside me?"

"Of course I can."

"Who are they?"

"Well let's see; for one thing there's Lie, and of course you lie a lot and refuse to believe. Then you have Blasphemy because you don't trust, you don't believe anything, and you certainly don't believe in him, the one they call God. You have Selfishness and Ambition. You are a very ambitious person. You have all those inside you, and you haven't even noticed. You don't much care whether it does you any good, but there it is, all the same. You shrug off the Holy One, you are just not interested in God. But she," added the demon, pointing to the woman whose mouth it was using, "she is different. She belongs to the Holy One."

"What 'Holy One'?"

"The Lord God."

"You can say his name?

"Of course I can."

"It doesn't hurt you?"

"No, and besides, I have to go anyway, so now it doesn't affect me. He's the Boss, you know. We have to bow down to him even if we don't want to. If he is in charge here, we all have to go, every one of us, even the powerful princes."

"I see. Does that mean you are about to leave?"

"Yes, I have to go. We are trying to stay, but he wants ... he ... .Ugh.

"What do you mean? Who wants?"

"There is a name above all names, and in that name we cannot refuse. That One already defeated us on a cross. He won out over all of us and he trampled us right down. We used to own the whole world, we were so powerful; but he beat us and now he is the One. Of course, there's one more that stayed behind and still lives in her. It's the Holy Spirit. But mind you, we will not stop fighting. We are furious. We have the whole world in our hands, but we don't have her, or any others who call themselves his children. We've been here for years, but we just haven't been able to get control of her. So what if we have the whole world? That's not good enough. Take you, for example, I care nothing about you because you already belong to the Evil One. What I want is her life, we want this one, and also want those other ones," he grumbled, pointing to the two Christians in the room. "That's why we're still here, but I don't know for how much longer. It all depends on what He has to say."

"What do you mean? What 'who' has to say?"

"Jesus."

"Is he telling you to stay or to go?"

"He's telling us ... no, that's enough. I'm not authorized to say it. He is the only one who knows how long we can stay and who can stay, but that's for him to know, not me."

"Has he commanded Satan to go too?"

"Satan is the king, the King of Darkness."

"Yes, and has God commanded him to leave?"

"We can't stay in the people who are God's children."

"But what about Satan? Has he been told to leave?"

"It makes no difference because he has no place here. Satan has no power over God's children."

"He will leave too, then?"

"He's over there," it said, waving a hand in the air. "He has agents here, and we are a big crowd, but he is not here himself.

"The other day I heard him speaking through Inés."

"Who, Satan? Speaking through Inés, from inside her?" Now it was jeering at him.

"Why yes."

"Satan is not inside Inés," it said with a smirk. "Didn't I just tell you she's God's property? He can't get in. I'm talking from her mind, but they can't talk from inside her."

"What? Where are you speaking from?"

"I told you! From her mind. I am not **inside** her. This is where I work from, I torment her mind."

"You mean Satan can't be in her mind?"

"No, not Satan. Satan is an angel, our king, our leader."

"I would like to speak with him, if I may."

"Speak with him directly? Go ahead, start talking."

"You mean right now?"

"You belong to him, after all, and you can talk to him whenever you please."

"How should I do it?"

"Very simple. Everyone who does not have Jesus belongs to Satan. You don't need an appointment, you just talk to him. You live with him, you know, but she doesn't. Nor do the others who are in another dimension, that other world that belongs to him, the Almighty."

"But who was the one that claimed to be Satan a couple of weeks ago?" I interjected.

"Oh, that was Ménguelesh."

"He was pretending to be Satan?"

"Sure, that's who it is.

"**Was**, I mean, but he's gone now. I keep telling you! Satan has many agents and princes.

"But why did that spirit claim to be Satan?"

"It was trying to confuse you because there was a spirit of confusion."

"Is it gone now?"

"Yes, it is."

"Who's still there?"

"Let's see. Myself, Torment. Also Death, Murder, Suicide, Destruction, Self-Destruction, Fear and Obsession. That's the whole crowd, so now you know. You're going to regret it, though, because we are principalities.

"So when are they all leaving?" my unbelieving colleague inquired.

"Ah, that I do not know. I just don't know."

"Why hasn't Rita been able to get you out yet?"

"Rita can't do it by herself, it's only the Mighty One who can get us out."

"Well then, why hasn't he been able to get rid of you?"

"Now that's a good question, and I don't know the answer. I never will know because that's something only he knows. Ask him if you want to know, but don't ask me because I don't know."

"Where do all of you get your strength?"

"I can't tell you that."

"No? Why not?"

"You have no power to be asking questions and you have no authority. I've told you far too much as it is. I won't answer any more of your questions."

At that point I took over and proceeded with the deliverance process until the spirit of Torment was expelled.

Some people who work in deliverance believe that demons always lie, that we cannot believe anything they say, and therefore we should not allow them to speak. I am sharing this case, though, to show that demons do tell the truth if you first bind them in Jesus' name and then order them to speak the truth. This evil spirit, probably speaking against its own will, convincingly explained who it was and why it persisted in tormenting this Christian woman. It even spoke the truth regarding its subjection to Christ. In a sense, it would be safe to say that, compelled by God himself, this demon preached the Gospel to my non-Christian psychologist colleague.

CHAPTER 12

GEAN CARLO: THE DEFIANT ADULTERER

G ean Carlo is a married man, 27 years old. His family had insisted he come to see me and repeatedly told him he needed deliverance. From the moment he walked in, he made it clear that he did not believe in any of this. He was convinced I had brainwashed his relatives with all my talk about demons.

He stalked in defiantly, fully intending to prove it was all a hoax. I challenged him and suggested he submit to the process even though he didn't believe in it. I also expressed my admiration at the fact he had come to me at all, despite his convictions, and pointed out that God would accept this as a step in the right direction.

He was still defiant and said, "At any rate I hope I don't hurt you if something goes wrong, because last night I saw myself in a dream with my hands around your neck, and I had strangled you to death."

He was trying to intimidate me, but I told him not to worry about it and that many people who come for deliverance feel a strong urge to destroy me, but have never done me any harm. I assured him that I was under God's protection and that no one could hurt me in spite of their violent urges to strike me. I then started the session by inquiring a bit about his beliefs and his past.

"I don't believe in anything," he said, "and although there must be a God, I haven't seen any proof of it. I suppose you would have to figure out some way of getting close to him, but I have never been interested. I can't even listen to a sermon without questioning everything the preacher has to say. I've been told I'm Satan himself, in the flesh, and I don't try to deny it. Who knows? Maybe they're right.

"The first time I saw you, it gave me chills and I felt terrified. I forced myself to hold your gaze and made up my mind to come here and prove that this whole thing is a farce, a big show you put on to prove a point. I've been into everything, gnosticism, astral projection, drugs, mushrooms, reincarnation, women; and I don't believe anything anymore.

"Once when a friend of mine needed help, I pretended to cast out demons from her. She was in bad shape, so I talked to the spirits and told them to come out of her and into me. All her problems suddenly disappeared, and I didn't feel a thing.

"Anyhow, I'm the black sheep of the family and I make fun of all Christians. Twice I've been on the verge of divorce, but my family convinced me not to go through with it. They told me they would disown me. In the end I let it go, and I don't even know why. Maybe it was for the children and my male ego because I wouldn't like to split up with my wife and see her take off with another man.

"I've always loved the military. I'm part of a paramilitary group, and I love the training and the environment. When I was thirteen, I had a brain tumor and asked God to take it away. I was healed without any treatment, and my family said it was a miracle. I think the doctors made a mistake, though, because I don't believe that stuff. My mother says when I was born, God told her I was going to be a preacher. Can you imagine? A preacher! Poor old Mom, such a disappointment! Sometimes I wish I had gone ahead and died because I can't stand myself.

I asked if he was willing to proceed with the deliverance, and he replied, "Do whatever you want. I don't believe any of it, so if there are demons, they will have to prove it to me."

I asked whether I could invite my assistant to be present, as she often worked with me. I explained that she had gifts of discernment and revelation that often proved very useful in such cases. I clarified that, as he could tell, she had not been present listening to our conversation, so if she happened to mention anything we had said, God himself would have revealed it to her as a help in the deliverance.

He agreed, so I brought my assistant into the office and we began to pray for discernment. I put together a suggested list of demons drawn from my conversation with Gean Carlo, and she made a separate list based only on what God revealed to her spirit. We then compared the lists and found that they were consistent: spirits of confusion, doubt, unbelief, fear, rebellion, aggression, violence, rage, oppression, arrogance, ridicule, death, rejection, adultery, resentment, hatred, failure and resistance. We knew we were on the right path when we found that our two lists were so similar.

We had identified an impressive collection of demons, so we showed him our two lists and asked him to confirm whether they seemed to reflect his view of himself. He read them and said, "Well, if demons really did exist, these would certainly be mine."

A message from God popped into my mind for Gean Carlo. "My son, it is hard for you to kick against the goads; your arrogance and self-sufficiency are destroying you to the point that you wish you did not exist, but I am the One who gives good gifts to everyone -- life, air and all other things. I am the one who sets the time and place for you to exist."

I told this to Gean Carlo, but he said nothing. Then my assistant added, "God is telling me that he has given you gifts of evangelism, counseling, teaching, faith, mercy, intercession, love, service, healing and revelation through dreams."

All Gean Carlo managed to say was, "So many?" But I could see he was stunned.

"So," I said, "are you ready to confront those demons?"

"Might as well," he replied. "Go ahead and we'll see what happens."

I asked God to free him in spite of his many doubts, to accept my own faith and conviction in place of his and to overlook Gean Carlo's unbelief. I asked God to protect all three of us, our families and possessions, and then I bound the spirits and commanded them, in Jesus' name, to manifest themselves and to be orderly about it. I had no sooner said the words, than Gean Carlo began to perspire and tremble.

He opened his eyes in fright and whispered, "What am I doing here?"

"What are you feeling?" I asked.

"I feel awful," he said, "and I wish I hadn't come."

I explained that he was feeling a demon's manifestation, but that it was nothing to be afraid of, and although he was experiencing unpleasant sensations, he was not in danger of any real harm. I rebuked several spirits, and he began to squirm and twist in his chair.

"Why are you so uncomfortable, demon?" I asked the spirit. "You have been found out. Are you afraid?"

"You bitch!" it cried in a rage.

"Be still and come out of him," I commanded.

"No, no!" it howled several times.

"Yes, out you go, along with all the rest of your minions in there."

"No! He surrendered to us and now he is ours."

"He came here to be set free, and God is not going to let him down," I replied. "God does not fail anyone who places trust in him."

"It's not going to be so easy!" he yelled in a rage. "He will never come to belief because we won't let it happen."

"He believed enough to come here," I pointed out, "and that's the best he can do at this point. As for the rest, I am standing in for him with my faith and my authority to fight."

The word "adultery" came into my mind. "Spirit of Adultery," I said ...

"No!" cried Gean Carlo, "I wanted that one to be the very last! I'm afraid of what will happen if that one goes. I would have to leave my other women, and I can't do that yet."

"Spirit of Adultery," I said again, "You first. Out, in Jesus' name. You will go, and he will decide for himself what to do about these women, without your interference."

We fought that spirit for over an hour until it finally skulked away. We asked God to pour his own presence into the empty space left behind by that spirit, filling it so the demon could not return. It was late, so we decided to stop there and continue another day.

Two days later, Gean Carlo showed up looking for me at a gathering in my church, waited until the end of the service, and then told me he urgently needed my help. I asked a young man from the church to join me in a small side room to pray for him, and as I began to rebuke the spirits, Gean Carlo broke out in a trembling sweat. His body went rigid and he began to scream at the top of his voice. He could be heard through the whole building, and three more people hurried in to help.

Several of them began to utter words of knowledge, information revealed by God. One of the men asked Gean Carlo, "Have you ever been involved with drugs?"

"Yes," he answered.

"God is telling me that one of the spirits got into you when you took too many drugs. We have to pray about it."

We all joined together asking God to break the effect of his drug abuse, and we commanded the spirit to be gone. It left in a burst of angry howls.

Someone asked, "There is something you find very frightening, right?"

"Yes," Gean Carlos answered. "Cats." My brother once locked me into the bathroom with a cat when I was very small. I was terrified, and I have lived with that fear ever since."

We prayed for God to heal this fear of cats and then cast out the demon of fear.

Someone else asked him, "Were you involved with a person who practiced witchcraft?"

"Yes," replied Gean Carlo. "It was a woman, but she's deceased. For a long time now I have felt that I will die on the same date she did, maybe next year."

"We break this false prophecy in Jesus' name," I answered. "The Lord says, I *'foil the signs of false prophets and make fools of diviners'*" (Is 44:25). This prophecy is a lie and we release Gean Carlo from it. Spirit of Death, come out right now. In Jesus' name we cast you out of him."

The Spirit of Death retorted that it had a foothold and would not leave. I quickly addressed Gean Carlo. "I feel you must give up your paramilitary group if we are to get rid of this spirit. Your military training is teaching you to kill, and that feeds the spirit of death. That is where it gets its power."

"Oh no!" moaned Gean Carlo, "I don't want to. I love that organization and don't want to leave. I've wanted to be a soldier ever since I was a child, and it will be too hard for me. I suppose you're right, but I don't know how to do it. I just can't."

"If you make up your mind to leave," I told him, "you will find that God can give you the strength you need. He will make you into his own soldier."

"All right, here goes," he relented, and gathering courage, he went on, "God, I give up my military training. HELP ME!" The cry for help came from the very depths of his soul, and he wept bitterly as he said it.

His body twisted into painful contortions and he screamed violently. Some of the believers began to rebuke the spirit, others prayed and sang praises to God, and a woman read from the Bible. He continued to scream and shake for several hours until finally, at 12:30 p.m., the Spirit of Death was cast out. It was the last one to leave.

God told me to put my hands on Gean Carlo's feet and say, "I anoint these feet with the Gospel of Peace, for you will take My message to many people. They will see my power through your experience."

We closed in prayer, turning Gean Carlo's whole life over to God, body, mind and spirit, and we asked the Holy Spirit to descend upon him in fullness. Only a week later, Gean Carlo was preaching in a church and telling his story, he had left his mistresses and he had resigned from the paramilitary movement.

Today he is an active member of his church, and the Lord is using him to help others through the very gifts that had been revealed to him even before he went through deliverance. So it is that we see fulfillment of God's prophecy, whispered to his mother at the time of his birth. He had been born to serve God, and at last it was happening.

GEAN CARLO TELLS HIS STORY

From the time I was a child, I had been very open to the things of God. I grew up in a Christian home and had experienced physical healing on two different occasions, which had touched me deeply. At the age of ten I contracted meningitis. The physicians did not expect me to survive, but my family organized a chain of prayer and fasting, and in the end I was healed.

Two years later I was hospitalized with a brain tumor. The night before my scheduled surgery, I cried out and told God that if he healed me, I would dedicate my life to serve him. That night God spoke to me and said he was already healing me and that I would go home the next day. That's exactly what happened. The doctors examined me the next morning, and their tests found no tumor, so I went home.

I can't explain how I managed to stray so far from God after being that close to him and being healed miraculously twice. That is exactly what happened, though, as I began to rebel against the church, religion in general and God above all.

As I raced after new experiences, I drifted into the hippie movement with its talk of peace, drugs, indolence and free sex, and it all became part of my lifestyle. Afterward I turned to gnosticism, yoga, transcendental meditation and oriental religions in general. None of it was enough, and I dabbled in every new thing that came along. I learned about astral projection, out-of-body experiences, mind control and encounters with so-called extraterrestrial beings. I was destroying myself slowly but surely, headed for total disaster. I will never know what held my marriage together.

One evening my wife and I were enjoying a family dinner at my parents' house when the conversation turned to the subject of demonic deliverance, and several family members shared their own personal experiences. They said they had been set free, they felt much better, and they mentioned a Rita Cabezas who had ministered to them in deliverance.

I was overcome with rage as I listened, and I began to make fun of them. "How could you let yourselves be so brainwashed with this nonsense?" I demanded. "Believe me, I have been into everything and can tell you there is no such thing as demons. And this Rita ... what a fake! She makes a few suggestions, and you fall right in line. How can you be so naive?"

No matter what I said, they seemed convinced, and although deep down I had to admit that they were visibly changed, I could never accept their claims of being set free from demons. Right then and there I resolved to put an end to these fairy tales, and I made it my goal to unmask this charlatan who called herself a Christian psychologist.

Only a few days later, I came into contact with a girl who confided in me. She described her problems, how bad she was feeling, and her suspicion that she was being tormented by evil spirits. I decided to go along with her story.

"If you think you are being harassed by demons, I can get rid of them for you. I'm not afraid of them and they can't do anything to me because I grew up being a Christian."

I sat in front of her and talked to the spirits, ordering them to leave her alone and pass into me. She immediately felt relief and began to weep with joy. "I feel so well now!" she exclaimed.

I felt happy for her and thought, "Well! That's certainly an easy trick, just the power of suggestion." Even so, as she left, I found that I was deeply fatigued, as if I had picked up a heavy load. "It's nothing at all," I thought. "I must have been concentrating really hard, and I wore myself out."

Some time later, for reasons I no longer recall, my parents, my wife and I visited the church Rita attended. I was very moved by the music they played in the service, and for the first time in many years I felt like joining in with the songs that still lingered in the memories of my childhood. I was puzzled by how much I was enjoying them.

The minister stood up and said, "God is showing me that several of you have severe headaches. He wants to heal you, so if you stand up, we will pray with you. Indeed, as three people rose to their feet, others gathered around them and began to pray.

"And the games begin!" I said to myself. "How can these people be so gullible and swallow all this? Any group this big will always have a few people with headaches. It's only reasonable, and no one needs divine revelation to figure it out. I could stand up myself and claim that God is telling me someone has a stomachache, and they would all jump to their feet too. It's just ridiculous!"

As they were praying for each other, another a woman went to the front and said, "There is a message here for someone who is grieving. Jesus would say to you, '*The Spirit of the Lord is upon you, because he has anointed you to comfort the afflicted. He has sent you to bind up the broken-hearted, to bestow on those who grieve a crown of beauty instead of ashes, the oil of gladness instead of mourning, and a garment of praise instead of despair.'* He would also say, *'I will comfort you. I will turn your tears into gladness, and the joy I give you will be far greater than your pain.'"*

My wife nudged me and said, "That's Rita."

I felt my face burning and I was seized with sensations of fear, fury and an urge to kill her. I was baffled and wondered what had come over me. "Come on, introduce us," I said to my mother, I want to meet her." What I really wanted was to confront her.

My mother walked me to where she was sitting and introduced me. Rita was very sweet and friendly with me, but I started to stare her down, driven by a strong feeling of revulsion and a desire to tear her apart. Oddly enough, even as I felt great hatred for her, I was also fearful. I was trembling inside and had to suppress the urge to dash out the door. I turned to leave, irritated and angry, and found her presence unbearable.

A few days later I said to my father, "Get me an appointment with Rita Cabezas, but don't tell anyone."

He was thrilled, thinking I had finally understood that I needed help. How could he have known my real motivations? The only reason I wanted to meet her was to get back at her for all the lies she had told my family. I hated her and wanted to show both her and my family that everything she was spouting about demons was a lie.

It did not cross my mind that I had another unconscious reason for setting that appointment. I still clung to a faint hope that what she said was true and had come just in time for her to help me. I see that now, but at the time I was not aware of it.

I showed up at the appointed time only to find that she was not ready for me; she said my appointment was not for another week, and that my father had gotten the right day of the week and the right time, but the wrong date.

I was beside myself, thinking, "This woman has figured me out. She knows I am here to expose her lies and now she's afraid to face me."

I decided not to go back, thinking, "I am not wasting another minute on her."

Somehow, though, even as my decision took shape, I felt a torrent of hopelessness crashing over me as my mind was bombarded with feelings of despair. "It's all over, and God is finished with me. Here I gave up my valuable time when I should have been at work, and she turns me away. That's it, this is all over."

But then I wondered, "Why am I thinking these things?" That's when I realized that deep down inside, I truly hoped she could help me dig my way out of this pit. I knew I was sick of the way I was living and I had had enough.

I continued to agonize over whether to attend my appointment with Rita, and I was torn with ambivalence. I gradually became more aware of the flood of conflicting emotions tugging me in every possible direction. While I was wracked with hostility and wanted to destroy Rita, I was also convinced that she was just a fake. Part of me was terrified of her, while at the same time, I had a deep-rooted desire to let her help me.

I was greatly torn by these two contrary drives, but at last I decided to show up at her office. As I waited outside for her to see me, a voice insisted, "Just get out of here! This is a waste of time, there's no point being here, and it's not worth it." But I decided to stay anyway.

At last the door opened and she asked me in, but as I entered, somewhere inside I felt trapped. I told Rita that my whole family had wanted me to go through deliverance, that I was the black sheep of the family and they were all worried about me. I also hastened to explain that I didn't believe in demons anyway and wasn't really sure whether I even believed in God.

We discussed these things until she asked, "It's clear that you don't believe in demons, but I'm wondering. If they really did exist, would you care whether there were any inside you? Would it matter at all if you knew for a fact that your desire for drugs, alcohol and women was caused by demons?"

"No," I answered, "of course not. If I believed there really were demons inside me I would want someone to take them out; but the fact is that neither you nor anyone else can convince me that they exist or hypnotize me or induce me into believing it."

"Good enough," she replied, "so I have a suggestion and I dare you to put me to the test. You prove to me that they don't exist, and I prove to you that they do. You're so dead set on it that you have nothing to lose, and if there are no demons, I'm the one who'll look like a fool. What do you say?"

"Fine with me," I answered. "You do your usual thing, I'll sit here with my eyes closed, and we'll see what happens."

When she began to pray, the whole exercise started getting harder for me as I saw in amazement that it was all happening just as my family had said it would. I realized that a strange force was rising up within me and taking over, and

I couldn't believe what I was feeling. The force took over my voice to answer Rita's questions, and I could do nothing to stop it. I was terrified and wanted to run away in panic, but my body was no longer under my own control and simply didn't respond.

Strange personalities vied for control and I felt a rush of powerful emotions: rage, weeping, pain, sadness, despair, ridicule. It was as if an army of negative creatures was battling inside me, trying to get me to leave, until a very clear voice spoke into my mind and said, "Stand up and get out of here."

Another voice urged me to stay, saying, "Keep going, and at the end of this you will find healing and freedom. I will uphold you."

I decided to go with the second voice, and I fought with all my strength to gain control over my mind and my mouth. Whenever I was able, I cried out to God, "If you are really here, help me!"

I struggled mightily as all my ideas and beliefs fell apart, and finally I said to myself, "So it's true. Demons are real and so is God. Both sides are speaking to my mind and I can hear them as if they were people. But that's impossible!" I didn't quite believe it.

The physical sensations I experienced were horrifying and I felt miserable. Thinking I was going to die right then and there, I said to God, "If I really am going, I want to die with you and not end up in hell with all these beasts. Take me, God, whether for life or for death."

At the end of the session, when it was all over and I was preparing to leave, I felt content, as if I had dropped a heavy load. My body was limp and weak, but my spirit had come back to life and I felt stronger on the inside. I spent many hours reflecting on what had happened that morning. Some of the thoughts in my mind told me I had been a fool to let myself be tricked just like the rest of my family, but another corner of my mind assured me that what I had experienced was real and would lead me to truth.

I looked up my lovers and told them it was over, that it had to end, that I had given my life over to Jesus and had been changed. I asked them to forgive me for the types of relationships I had sustained with them and that I knew I had hurt them. I wept and ached with each one, not wanting to leave them but knowing that it was in obedience to God's will. If it had been up to me, I wouldn't have done it because I was truly fond of them and wanted to go on seeing them. But God had spoken very clearly, and I knew I had to break it off.

It was the most difficult thing I've ever done, as I was so used to having them in my life that they had become a part of me. I fell into a deep depression, not knowing what would become of my life or how I was going to get along without them.

"So you think you can get rid of them," taunted a jeering voice. "And how do you plan to fill the empty space they leave behind? What do you intend to do with all the time you used to spend with them? Who can you have fun with now? And what about the one who's pregnant with your child? When your wife finds out she'll leave you. So do you still think it will do you any good to give your life to God? It looks to me like now you have more problems now than ever before."

The taunts tore at my heart, and I was tormented by the memory of that first deliverance session. I could not stand the idea of having to go through it again, but even though it had been so tough, something kept telling me I had to finish what I had started.

A gathering was scheduled at the church two days later, and I assumed Rita would be there. I considered going so I could follow through on my deliverance and get it over with as quickly as possible because the anxiety was killing me. I asked God to speed it all up because I was truly miserable.

I spent all day Saturday fighting with myself. A very powerful force inside me tried to dissuade me from going to the church, wielding every possible argument. Another force fought back, urging me to go and promising me victory. I stepped out of the car to go into the church, and every step I took was a major feat as the fierce battle raged inside me. I made it through the door and was soon assailed by overwhelming feelings of loneliness, fear, discouragement and anxiety.

"This process will never end," I moaned. "Someone else more important than me will show up, and Rita won't have time for me. She will never get around to me, so I might as well just leave and stop wasting my time. I have waited too long to start following God, and now I will never be able to change."

The swirl of wild thoughts raged on in my mind as the church service progressed. It finally ended after what seemed like a lifetime, and the people who wanted prayer were divided into groups.

Even though I had sat through the service for an hour and a half, now I began to hesitate. "Should I go up, or just leave? And if Rita decides she can't see me today, what will I do? It would be the end of me because I need this now and can't tolerate the situation any longer."

It took all my strength just to stand up and approach Rita, frightened and timid as I was. My attitude as I walked toward her had undergone a dramatic change, for my earlier wall of hostility and rebellion was simply gone.

"Do you think you could pray for me a little?" I asked hesitantly.

"Of course," she said. "Let's go into the side room so we can have some privacy."

Such a sense of relief that she hadn't turned me away! So that was the start of my second deliverance session.

If I had known what awaited me that night, I probably would never have set foot inside the church. The demon manifested, as expected, and it was ten times worse than on the first go-round. A spirit roared out of hiding, took possession of me and forced me to scream obscenities I never wanted to say. I howled like a wild animal and my body went rigid as my muscles tightened into spasms. I truly believed I was dying and feared I might kill someone. A force was trying to strangle me and I could hardly breathe.

Several other people had now come in to help Rita, and when I was finally able to talk, I begged them not to leave me like that, but to press on until everything had been cast out. "My God, my God," I cried, "have your way with me! Do whatever you need to do! Just let me be sure I am back with you and we are reconciled."

That was when I began to feel some relief, as if Satan had released his hold at that very instant. I began to sense a deep peace such as I had never known before. A beautiful song rose up within me, a song I had never heard, and it began to flow out through my mouth. The others were singing along with me, and we were all united in holy worship.

It seemed strange that my hands were raised, as if trying to reach God, suspended in the air, held up by a force I could not see. A pleasant warmth seeped into my hands and head and flooded down into my whole being. A pure sense of joy bubbled up from the depths of my soul, a joy such as I had never experienced. At the same time, I felt like I was immersed in a pool of gladness and well-being and that my life was finally worth living.

I was experiencing a fullness of life that was new to me. I saw how wonderful it was to be a Christian, and I understood that placing myself in God's hands was precious and holy. God's spirit moved within me as he whispered, "You are my son. I am cleansing you, healing you and setting you free. I am preparing you for my service."

"Lord," I answered, "do whatever you wish with my life. Just give me the strength to get through the rest of this deliverance and the courage to follow you and do your will."

After this brief pause, the battle started again and I felt another demon coming up. It crashed through with a screech as it named itself: a spirit of death. There were many ties binding it to me, and I had to give them all up. The hardest one to let go of was all my special paramilitary training.

"Lord God," I sighed, "you know I don't want to give this up, but if I need to, I will. I only ask that you give me the strength."

I had to renounce it aloud, and the demon went wild and threatened to kill me. It wracked my whole body with convulsions, and I screamed over and over from the unbearable pain. Something was being torn out of me and ripping me apart as it let go. Each scream sent something flying out through my mouth, invisible but very real.

The deliverance I had been longing for was finally complete, and God flooded through my body, my mind and my spirit as he suffused me with his presence. I felt a great relief, light as a feather, clean and even honorable. The burden of my atrocious past had been lifted off my shoulders and I promised myself I would never again wander away from God or do anything that might land me in another deliverance like this. I decided to safeguard the work God had done in me that night. I had learned that evil exacts a price that is too high to pay, and I knew I would never be able to do it again.

The process had been very embarrassing, and when God began to reveal the things of my past to all the people who were there praying with me, I felt more grotesque than the filthiest garbage. I wanted to vanish from the face of the earth. I pleaded for the ground to open up and swallow me as I suffocated under the weight of my own sins. It was an awful experience to have God revealing things that I believed no one else could possibly have known. I learned that night that God respects no secrets, and nothing can be hidden from him. His bright light in that place shone on all the wrongdoings I had committed in hiding.

I was totally demoralized, stripped naked before God and those who were faithfully serving as channels of his power. I understood, though, that none of it was intended to humiliate me or harm me, but rather to set me free me from it all. He did it to heal me and bless me, and after I was finally broken before him, he himself lifted me up with his love.

I died that night, and everyone who had known me before saw that the man they thought they knew had ceased to exist. The person who lives now is someone else altogether, because a new creature had risen up, a changed man.

It was nearly morning as I headed home, and I felt like a torrent of joy was gushing forth from my soul. I could scarcely contain it, it was wonderful, and I wanted only to serve God. Now I knew he really existed, he loved me, and this world offered nothing better than to be one with him. I discovered the delight of a lonely wanderer who travels the world for many long years aimlessly searching for a treasure and finally returns home to discover it was right there all along and is so much more precious than he had ever imagined.

The next day was Sunday, and I was the first one at church. I had developed an insatiable thirst for God and felt driven to make up for all the years I had squandered. I had discovered in the deliverance session what it was like to hear God's voice inside my mind, and although I was afraid it had been a one-time experience, I soon learned that there was more. I have continued to hear his voice, and he faithfully speaks to me when he sees fit. He has given me the gift of knowledge and has used me to help others find deliverance. I had made fun of the ministries I saw in action the first time I went to the church, but now he chose to give me those very same giftings. God does have a sense of humor, that's for sure!

I am currently enrolled in a theological seminary, studying to help others to find the way forward just as I did, through God's grace, back when this all started. I pray that God will raise up more people in the ministries of deliverance and inner healing, because the need is so great and the workers are so few. If God uses my experience to reach others, may it be for his glory. Hallelujah! God is real, he lives, and I live in him.

CHAPTER 13

SANDY: DISSOCIATIVE IDENTITY DISORDER

S andy had been in treatment with three different psychiatrists for close to ten years when she came to me for help. She had come from the United States and had a primary diagnosis of dissociative identity disorder[3] and a secondary diagnosis of manic-depressive disorder.

When we first met, she suffered from an extremely high state of anxiety. She would sit down, stand up, walk around the room, look out the window, express a desire to push her hand through the glass, hide her face in her hands, sit down again, fidget around in her chair and so on. Verbal expression was very difficult for her. She spoke in incoherent bursts and was unable

3 DISSOCIATIVE IDENTITY DISORDER: formerly known as Multiple Personality Disorder, a mental condition whose sufferer reports two or more alternating personality states.

to articulate complete thoughts. She was very confused, fearful and depressed.

She told me about her clinical history in psychiatry and recalled earlier times when she had seemed better able to control her emotions than at present. I shared my own sense of what I saw happening and briefly mentioned a few of my other cases that might resonate with her.

She listened as best she could in her confused state and answered, "Well, maybe some of my personalities are demons, but not all of them because some aren't evil at all, they're just children. My current psychiatrist has identified thirty so far, and some are very destructive and aggressive. Maybe those are demons."

"We can figure that out," I explained, "if you're willing to work with me through a process of spiritual deliverance."

She fidgeted around for a while, thought about my offer and finally said, "You have my permission, so go ahead and do what you normally do in these cases."

I bound the demons in her, in Jesus' name, and commanded them to manifest. I then witnessed an immediate transformation as an angrily defiant personality took over.

"Who are you?" I asked.

"I can tell you what she calls me," it cackled. "'Lucinda,' that's her name for me."

"No!" I interrupted, "I command you to give me your REAL name."

"Nope. Don't want to."

"But you must," I came back at it, "I command you to speak the truth, in Jesus' name."

Sandy came to herself at that point and started to moan, "My head feels like it's going to explode, I'm so confused. They're talking to my mind and saying they aren't demons, that they're my real personalities and I shouldn't have come here. They're trying to make me feel guilty because what I'm doing is wrong and I'm hurting them. They're telling me to go back home, back to my psychiatrist. I'm too confused, we should just stop because I can't go on with this. I'm so sorry, I have to go and catch the first plane home because I need my psychiatrist."

I told her that I would certainly not work with her against her will, and although I did not recommend it, she was free to leave if she chose. "I'll be here if you change your mind," I offered.

So my friend Ana, who had brought Sandy in the first place, drove her home. Ana told me later that she had to fight with the demons all the way to Sandy's house because they were manifesting in the car and pushing Sandy to leap out of the car and kill herself.

Sandy's aunt was alarmed when they reached the house and she saw the state Sandy was in, and she told Ana, point blank, that she opposed spiritual deliverance and would allow no further communication from Ana. "Don't even call her on the phone," she said to Ana. "I will not allow you to speak to her any more. I am responsible for my niece while she is in this country and I will see to it that you do her no further damage. Here I thought you would be a friend, you would help her, but now I don't trust you."

When Ana told me this, I became very concerned for two reasons. First, I was worried about Sandy and what would become of her. The demons had openly threatened to make her kill herself and had already succeeded several times in pushing her into suicide attempts. My second fear was for my own professional standing. Sandy's uncle was a physician deeply opposed to the practice of spiritual deliverance. He believed none of it and was in a position to get me into serious trouble if he wanted to.

"Lord," I prayed, "please protect my reputation. This doctor could be a real threat to me, and I cannot handle it on my own, Father. Please take this problem off my hands."

Ana and I organized several prayer chains to intercede for Sandy and ask God to take direct action. "God," I poured out my heart, "if it is your will for me to minister deliverance to her, open the door that has just been shut. You are the God of the impossible, specialized in situations just like this one. The more impossible it seems, the better, because the world will know that your power alone swept away every obstacle so your name might be glorified."

As I said this, a passage from the book of Revelation (3:7-8, 13) came to mind: *"These are the words of him who is holy and true, who holds the key of David. What he opens no one can shut, and what he shuts no one can open. I know your deeds. See, I have placed before you an open door that no one can shut. I know that you have little strength, yet you have kept my word and have not denied my name. ... Whoever has ears, let them hear what the Spirit says to the churches."*

I found a Bible to look it up, and I gasped out loud when I saw who the message was addressed to – the church in Philadelphia! I myself was born in Philadelphia, Pennsylvania! "Thank you, God for making this message so personal, just for me.

Ana began calling Sandy to talk while her aunt was away at work, but Sandy was still very upset. Her aunt had taken her to a Roman Catholic priest who assured her that her ailments were clearly psychiatric in nature and had nothing to do with demons. Sandy was a faithful Catholic and knew she should submit to his request that she stay away from spiritual deliverance. He was a priest, after all, and he must know.

"Please don't try to talk to me," she remonstrated. "I'm too confused and I don't know whether you and Rita are right. Please leave me alone. I'm going back home this week because I need my psychiatrist."

Our prayer group of intercessors for Sandy redoubled our supplications. "Lord," we pleaded, "please do something fast because time is running out." God's intervention finally came, although he withheld his answer until the very last moment, as he so often does. I don't much care for his timing, but I have to admit that it bolsters my faith.

"Rita," came Ana's excited voice over the telephone, "I just talked to Sandy. She has decided to stay in Costa Rica and says things are starting to clear up in her mind. She is hesitantly willing to believe us even though she doesn't fully understand. She says God had spoken to her when she was still in California and told her to come to Costa Rica, that something good was going to happen here. She now admits that it was her deliverance and says God is telling her to stay here and not go back home until he tells her to. He said that He will work in her a change so striking that she will be able to testify to many people, including her current psychiatrist, about her deliverance. Sandy wants to start as soon as we can, but we need to find a time when her aunt is away at work and can't stop her."

"Praise the Lord! I shouted, nearly bursting Ana's eardrum, and I felt like tossing the phone into the air. I had almost given up, but God was faithful and had kept his promise.

I recalled certain passages from Habakkuk, showing me he was in control of the situation: "*How long, Lord, must I call for help, but you do not listen?*" (Hab 1:2). "*Look at the nations and watch—and be utterly amazed. For I am going to do something in your days that you would not believe, even if you were told*" (Hab 1:5). "*Then the Lord replied: Write down the revelation ... For the revelation awaits an appointed time ... it speaks of the end and will not prove false.* Though it linger, wait for it; it will certainly come and will not delay" **(Hab 2:2-3).**

We all met together again only a few days after that phone conversation, to get started on Sandy's deliverance. As the face-off began, the demons were very reluctant to relinquish the information I was demanding, but little by little they revealed their footholds.

"What is your real name?" I asked the demon.

"Sordoloquith."

"How did you get in?"

"It was at the county hospital, when a group of psychiatrists and nurses from a satanic cult got hold of her and dedicated her to Satan. They had just revived her from a suicide attempt, so they took her to the hospital basement around midnight, on Monday and Tuesday, October 16 and 17, 1975. They sacrificed a pig, a dog and a cat, and sprinkled her with the blood.

They killed the animals right in front of her, but she was only half conscious. Her eyes were mostly closed, and although they roused her from time to time, she was only half there. After they had anointed Sandy with the animal blood, they daubed urine on her hands and forehead."

"Keep talking!" I commanded, pressing the demons for more information.

"There was a corpse. Her own psychiatrist, the high priest that night, gouged out the corpse's eyes and ate them. There was a rattlesnake in a cage and they fed it human flesh cut from the corpse as a symbol of human life offered to Satan, and they gave it animal flesh too.

"There was also a small garter snake that they placed on top of Sandy. It coiled around her neck, wrists and ankles and then slithered all over her naked body. The idea was to force her into submission by terrifying her and then deliver her up to Satan and to us. They offered her to Satan to be his high priestess."

"Wait!" I interrupted, "Doesn't that require voluntary submission?"

"They were supposed to have gotten it," answered the demon. "Her psychiatrist tried over and over again to get her to deny her belief in God, but she refused to say it out loud. He drugged her and hypnotized her and tried to break her will, but she wouldn't let go. She's marked, though, with Satan's sign on the palm of her left hand–a red five-pointed star inside a black circle. You can't see it normally, but it comes into sight whenever she hears the sound of a Black Mass. They traced it on her hand with blood."

Three of us were ministering to Sandy, and we all placed our open hands face-down on her left palm and broke the power of the satanic mark and then cleansed her from it by invoking the blood of the Lamb of God. As we did this, Sandy's body shook with horrible sensations. We asked the demon if the mark had been removed, and it reluctantly assented.

"She was programmed under hypnosis," explained Sordoloquith, "to forget everything that happened those two nights."

That was when Sandy came to and said she was afraid to continue. "I can feel all the demons inside me," she cried in terror. "They are all over my body and I'm afraid they will take control completely and I won't be able to stop myself. They hate you, Rita, and they want to strike you."

"Don't worry about that," I assured her, "they can't hurt me. They can try anything, but it won't work because I am under God's protection."

"But I'm afraid because I can't tell whether they are telling you the truth. I think they are, but I'm not sure."

"Sandy, you are doing fine," I replied, "so let us take care of discerning and don't you worry about it. At this point you are too confused to tell the difference, so just give them your permission to manifest. Right now we need whatever information they can give us so we can reverse all the damage they have done."

One of the missionaries present, George Weinand, prayed for God's assurance that He was protecting her. Then his wife Gayle said, "Sandy, you need to understand that you are laying bare a towering hierarchy in the devil's army, and we can't get it done unless you are willing to let them manifest and tell us everything. They cannot hurt you, but you need to fight through. God says, 'When you pass through the waters, I will be with *you; and when you pass through the rivers, they will not sweep over you. When you walk through the fire, you will not be burned; the flames will not set you ablaze. For I am the Lord your God, the Holy One of Israel, your Savior'* (Is 43:2-3)."

"Remember that we are right here protecting you and we will not leave you alone. Try to understand that for many people, the road to deliverance leads through the heart. We are the bridges on that road, and we have stretched our own bodies over those stormy waters so you can cross over. We are here to help you through this, no matter how long it takes."

"All right," murmured Sandy, "let's do it. I command you demons to speak, because you want me to think this is coming from my own unconscious mind, but I know it isn't."

"That's right, Sordoloquith," I interjected. "Speak now, in the name of Jesus. What else do we need to know to break your power? Tell us exactly what they said in the dedication ceremony," I ordered.

"Every section of her body was dedicated to Satan so she could be used for destruction. She was subjected to sexual acts with the people there, all the men and all the women. They also used dismembered parts of the corpse for sexual acts with her body. They were getting her ready for the same things they were doing, so she could bring people to Satan. She would seduce if seduction was needed or inflict pain disguised as kindness, all for hidden purposes. She would be used to commit murder when necessary, just as they did, and serve as an instrument of war and hatred. Go ahead and laugh, but believe that it's true even if it's not on a large scale, because small jobs are just as important. She was going to perform everything imaginable, if we could only get her to submit." The demon fell silent.

"Keep talking!" I demanded.

"I want to kill you," it snarled.

"Too bad for you that you can't," I retorted. "Go on."

"If Sandy says so, we can go on."

"Sandy does not need to give you more permission because she has chosen to place herself under God's control, as you know perfectly well. It was her conscious decision and you cannot reverse it."

"But we can certainly try," the demon snickered.

"Kind of like when you tried to take God's throne, but that didn't work out too well for you either. His power is far greater than yours, so tell me," I went on, "do these people do the same things to other patients, that they did to Sandy?"

"Yes, because after all, don't doctors and nurses always have access to corpses and patients?"

That morning we failed to get any more information from the demon, but it came out later. Sandy showed undeniable improvement over the three months we worked with her, and we will press on until she is fully delivered.

The key message from this case is that Satan has infiltrated the staff of a psychiatric hospital and he could easily be doing more of the same in other facilities.

Therefore God is asking, "Are any of my sons and daughters willing to serve as instruments of my power to do battle against Satan's strategy? These professional psychiatrists have let themselves be used in Satan's service, so where are my people willing to work for me in the same field?"

Satan needs to be exposed and unmasked and God needs Christian warriors. The Lord is asking, "Whom shall I send? And who will go for us? Is anyone willing to answer as Isaiah did, 'Here I am; send me?'"

CHAPTER 14

DEMONS AND THE PRACTICE OF PSYCHOLOGY

M any readers may feel puzzled by the title of this chapter. "The two concepts are complete opposites, so what can they have in common?" you may wonder. The pairing is perfectly valid in my view.

Dating back to medieval times, emotional disturbances were often erroneously diagnosed as demon possession. Endless forms of cruelty were applied to people who displayed abnormalities, in the belief that the demon dwelling in the body could be rendered so uncomfortable that eventually it would depart.

The growing science of human behavior changed these views, offering more rational and humane approaches to treatment. As the profession evolved, all notions of demon possession were eventually expunged in the interest of science.

Certain Christian psychologists are beginning to disagree, having rediscovered the ancient diagnosis of demonization. I have personally investigated hundreds of cases of disorders that did not respond to psychological treatments but were eliminated by spiritual methods, giving our team clear evidence that certain pathologies are indeed introduced and sustained by evil spirits.

The Bible unambiguously describes numerous cases of demonization and distinguishes them from physical or mental illness. Matthew 4:24 says, "*News about him spread all over Syria, and people brought to him all who were ill with various diseases, those suffering severe pain, the demon-possessed, those having seizures, and the paralyzed; and he healed them.*"

Although many psychologists have concluded that these episodes narrated in the Bible are actually cases of mental illness misunderstood under the primitive state of scientific knowledge, I disagree. I think those early writers knew exactly what they were talking about. The same types of events and strange behaviors are still happening today. Modern-day sufferers turn first to psychologists and psychiatrists, but when treatment attempts fall short and patients fail to improve, they desperately seek out the few churches that still practice spiritual deliverance.

I am convinced that more psychologists should be investigating this phenomenon, as it is more frequent than they realize and is intimately linked to their profession. They would be astonished if they gave it a chance and, sitting in on deliverance sessions or "exorcisms", as identified in the Catholic church, could see for themselves how dramatically the patients' personalities change and how clearly the demons describe themselves as destructive spirits spewing out contempt for God. They would also observe patients exhibiting supernatural strength when the demon manifests itself and would easily pinpoint the very instant when it departs the body, leaving the person completely free of its influence and restored to a normal state that remains long after the session ends.

These events can be very moving, and for those who are not prepared for them, terrifying. Bizarre things may happen, impossible to explain from a strictly scientific or rational perspective, so that most people cannot sit in on such sessions without becoming convinced that something supernatural is going on. They tend to be amazed above all by the fact that no external devices or straitjackets are needed to restrain patients. The evil spirits are simply ordered to be gone, and out they go from the patient's body, albeit raging in anger, grumbling and resisting, until the person is completely healed in the affected area. Healing occurs because the command to go, uttered in

Jesus' name, brings to bear his full authority. The only way to help people who are under demonic influence is by recognizing that demons really do exist, understanding how they work and learning to confront them.

Unclean spirits did not vanish from the face of the earth just because psychology decided to strike the word "demon" from its scientific lexicon. Demons are still doing their destructive work, although today they act with a much freer hand than ever before because so few people know how to identify them or, even less, how to confront them. Now that we have rediscovered them, though, we can finally start to improve on medieval methods for removing them, so it is time to take up this mission once again and carry it forward.

WHAT ARE DEMONS?

Demons are evil spirits intent on destroying human beings by separating them from their creator. While they do not possess physical bodies, they do have very distinct personalities. They can enter people's minds or bodies, where they produce mental, emotional, bodily or behavioral disorders.

Theologians interpret the Bible passages in Isaiah 14:12-14 and Ezekiel 28:11-19 as telling the story of Satan's fall. According to these texts, Satan, the devil, is the leader of all unclean spirits and originally served as one of God's archangels, probably the most powerful being in his service. He eventually became puffed up with pride and aspired to be equal to God, refusing to submit and claiming the creator's position for himself.

The human heart mirrors this same sin whenever it embraces humanism and refuses to recognize that we were created by God and cannot live without him. The claim of humanism is that we can take God's place for ourselves, ignoring the fact that no created being can exist apart from its creator.

Satan's rebellion against God attracted other angels to join him, and when they refused to submit to his sovereign authority, God cast them from heaven onto this earth. This is why Jesus said, "I saw Satan fall like lightning from heaven" (Lk 10:18). They have been trying ever since to establish their kingdom here on earth, which is why the Bible describes Satan as "the god of this age" (2 Co 4:4).

The book of Ephesians points to this same army when it says, "Put on the full armor of God, so that you can take your stand against the devil's schemes. For our struggle is not against flesh and blood, but against the rulers, against the authorities, against the powers of this dark world and against the spiritual forces of evil in the heavenly realms" Eph 6:11-12.

How do demons get in?

People may fall under demonic influence or invasion in many different ways:

1. **Traumatic experiences.** Victims of rape, serious accidents, being attacked or bitten by dogs, hospital stays, a history of childhood abandonment or abuse, and the like.

2. **Sin.** People may have committed adultery, stealing, lying, abortion, idolatry (refusing to give God first place in their lives), holding grudges, and so forth.

3. **Curses.** Curses may be administered by means of witchcraft or black magic, or it could be as simple as saying something apparently harmless like "Damn you!" or "I hope you break your leg," or "You good-for-nothing, you will never get anywhere." Parents often program their children with these negative life scripts, never even considering the psychological and spiritual power their own words may possess.

4. **Heredity.** God says in Exodus 20:5 that those who hate him will see their sin punished through their children, grandchildren and great-grandchildren, meaning that children may pay for their parent's sins and mistakes. Parents under demonic influence expose

their children to similar influence, such that a man bound by a spirit of fear may pass on his fear to one or more of his children. In another example, a woman may have made a pact with Satan because she was infertile and wanted to have children, but her offspring will end up having to pay the price. Even birth outside of marriage (fruit of fornication) could be an open door for demons.

5. **Occult practices.** People or their close friends or family may be involved in occult practices, often out of ignorance or in "fun", such as playing with a Ouija board, and such practices may introduce them to demonic influence. Demons seize any opportunity available to invade a life.

6. **Contamination of the physical senses.** This could mean the use of drugs, pornography, horror movies, satanic rock music, etc.

No need to fear

The Bible teaches that believers should be on the lookout for demon attacks, and this has erroneously filled many Christians with unnecessary fear. Jesus assured his followers, "*I have given you authority to trample on snakes and scorpions and to overcome all the power of the enemy; nothing will harm you. However, do not rejoice that the* spirits submit to you, but rejoice that your names are written in heaven" (Lk 10:19-20).

He also said, "Very truly I tell you, whoever believes in me will do the works I have been doing, and they will do even greater things than these, because I am going to the Father" (Jn 14:12). The book of Matthew narrates several incidents in which Jesus successfully confronts demons and forces them out of their victims (Mt 8:28-33, Mt 9:32-33, Mt 15:22-28 and Mt 17:15-21). This means that all those who believe in Jesus as the son of God have the same power and therefore have no reason to fear the devil. Christians are equipped to fight him and make him flee, which is why the apostle Peter said, "*Be alert and of sober mind. Your enemy the devil prowls around like a roaring lion looking for someone to devour. Resist him, standing firm in the faith, because you know that the family of believers throughout the world is undergoing the same kind of sufferings*" (1 Pe 5:8-9). James, in a similar statement, says "*Submit yourselves, then, to God. Resist the devil, and he will flee from you*" (Jas 4:7).

SYMPTOMS OF DEMONIC ATTACK

The Bible's portrayals of demonic attack reveal a variety of symptoms. The gospel of Mark (Mk 5:1-20) tells the story of a man who modern-day psychologists would have diagnosed as psychotic, living in isolation among the tombs and ferociously attacking all passersby. Townspeople had tried to restrain him, but he was so strong that he snapped all their chains. His moans could be heard night and day throughout the surrounding hillsides, and his body was bruised from self-inflicted beatings with stones. He perfectly fits today's definition of psychosis, a person not in control of his own mind who has lost all contact with reality.

Jesus ordered the demons to leave this man and gave them permission to enter a herd of pigs. The two thousand pigs stampeded down a hill and over the edge of a cliff and drowned in the lake, upon which the man recovered his senses.

Many people have wondered why Jesus allowed the demons to enter the herd of pigs. I believe his intent was to show the witnesses to the incident that something real, something destructive had indeed been present in this man and that it departed physically before entering the pigs and killing them. Certainly no one can claim that the pigs were subject to suggestion or victims of hysteria, both of which could have been human reactions. They had no understanding of what was happening. Something unquestionably evil got into them and led them to their deaths, which is exactly what would have happened eventually to the man of the tombs, had it not been for Jesus. This, in my view, is clear proof that unclean spirits are a reality.

Other passages describe a variety of symptoms in their accounts of demonic action. A victim in Matthew 9:32-34, possessed by a mute spirit, regains the ability to speak the instant the spirit is driven out. A spirit described in Matthew 12:22 causes blindness and deafness. Mark 9:14-29 is the story of a boy affected by spirits that cause epileptic-type seizures and self-destructive behaviors that leave him deaf and mute. His seizures often expose him to dangerous situations, throwing him into water or fire. Luke 13:10-16 tells of a spirit of infirmity that severely cripples a woman to the point that her back is bent over double. A woman in Acts 16:16-18 is controlled by a spirit of divination.

Below is a list of spirits I have seen in my practice, that identified themselves by the type of ailment they produce.

Abandonment

Aggressiveness

Anguish

Anxietynce

Blockage

Condemnation

Confusion

Covetousness

Curses

Death

Deceitfulness

Defeatism

Depression

Destruction

Discouragement

Divination

Doubt

Escapism

Exhaustion

Fear

Gluttony

Greed

Guilt

Hatred

Helplessness

Homosexuality

Idolatry

Impatience

Insecurity

Insomnia

Irritability

Isolation

Jealousy

Laziness

Legion

Lewdness

Loneliness

Lust

Lying

Madness

Mockery

Murder

Nervousness

Oppression

Pain

Poverty

Pride

Rage

Rebelliousness

Rejection

Resentment

Resistance

Restlessness

Ruin

Sadness

Self-hate

Selfishness

Sexual perversion

Sorcery

Suicide

Theft

Torment

Unbelief

Unworthiness

Urge to flee

Vice

Violence

Weakness

Witchcraft

Because many of these names are clearly relevant to psychology, the suggestion that demons can cause such conditions as nervousness, insecurity, anxiety, depression, defeatism, madness, and the like, reveals how closely interconnected psychology is with theology. A modern-day sufferer such as the man living among the tombs would be taken to a professional. Who better than a psychiatrist or a psychologist to treat such a case? Professionals who know nothing about confronting demons, however, would probably write these patients off as "hopeless cases" to be institutionalized and drugged indefinitely.

Demons, though, will never succumb to electroconvulsive therapy, pills, or psychotherapy, and I challenge anyone who doubts this to give it a try. It will never work because demons leave only when they are brought face to face with a mature Christian speaking in the name of Jesus, and they simply laugh at psychologists who do not take a spiritual stance.

A demon once challenged me by saying, "Your psychology can't touch me and can never come against me." When I replied saying, "I am not fighting you as a psychologist but as a daughter of God," it ran out of arguments and had to go.

COMMON TARGETS OF DEMONIC ATTACK

1. The mind

2. The emotions

3. The body

4. Spiritual life including prayer, Bible reading and worship

5. The general environment, whether at home or in the workplace. The environment surrounding demonized persons may be affected in a number of ways: light bulbs explode for no apparent reason, objects move, doors and windows unexplainably open and close, strange shadows appear, rocks fall from nowhere inside a building, footsteps are heard although no one is in the building, furniture moves around, or there may be strange odors, abnormally low temperatures in the sufferer's bedroom, animals in places that offer no means of entrance, strange voices, and so forth, all for no apparent reason.

DETECTING A DEMON

The following circumstances may reveal the presence of a demon:

Direct observation of the affected person.

Experiences recalled by the sufferer or acquaintances.

Supernatural events, such as pictures on the wall moving about when the person enters a room, strange noises heard in the house, the bed shifting around in the night, etc.

Direct revelation by the Holy Spirit through the gift of discernment of spirits.

DISCERNMENT OF SPIRITS

This spiritual gift, cited in 1 Corinthians 12:10, is a God-given ability by which certain people can tell whether demons are present in a person, and if so, their names and qualities. The information is given to the person's spirit and mind by direct revelation of the Holy Spirit. Jesus appeared to be using this in the story narrated in Mark 9:14-29. A boy's father tells Jesus about his son's epileptic seizures, and when Jesus confronts the demon, he addresses it as, "You deaf and mute spirit, ... I command you, come out of him and never enter him again." The text gives no indication that anyone had told Jesus the boy was deaf or mute, but Jesus discerned it in his spirit.

CASTING OUT DEMONS

I strongly insist that only Christians should confront demons in Jesus' name, because the word "Jesus" is not simply a magic word that makes them go away. Demons know perfectly well who has authority to invoke the name of Jesus and who does not.

The Bible offers a specific illustration in the story of the Jewish exorcists, not followers of Jesus, who tried to cast out demons *"'In the name of Jesus whom Paul preaches'* ... *One day the evil spirit answered them, "Jesus I know, and Paul I know about, but who are you?"* *Then the man who had the evil spirit jumped on them and overpowered them all. He gave them such a beating that they ran out of the house naked and bleeding"* (Ac 19:13-16).

It is also important to stress that this kind of ministry should be practiced only by mature Christians. Some churches teach that any believer can do it, and although this is true in theory, I have seen unfortunate cases of demons passing into Christians present at the deliverance session who lacked sufficient spiritual stability to be fully protected by the Lord's presence. Such cases can be very sad because these believers sincerely wanted to help deliver their friends, but their good intentions were not enough to keep them out of harm's way. This is why I discourage inexperienced Christians from attempting to minister deliverance.

CONFRONTING A DEMON

No two cases are exactly alike, but the following basic steps generally apply in a deliverance session:

1. Open in prayer, asking God to protect everyone present, their families and

possessions, and asking him to anoint the deliverance.

2. Take authority in Jesus' name and bind all demonic forces.

3. Undo the demon's reluctance to manifest, in Jesus' name, and order it to come out from its hiding place, take control of the affected person's mouth, and answer all questions asked. Always bind it to truth so it cannot give false information.

4. Command the demon to identify itself by name. This is what Jesus did in Mark 5:1-20 above, when the demon replied, "*My name is Legion, for we are many.*" You have greater power over a demon if you know its name, which in turn tells you what part of the person has been affected so you can easily confirm afterward whether the area has in fact been freed.

5. Order the unclean spirit to identify its foothold so you can deal with and destroy it in Jesus' name.

6. Pray for God to heal painful memories, especially if the demons have identified them as footholds.

7. Cut all detrimental spiritual heritages from mother, father and ancestors.

8. Destroy the power of any witchcraft, curses or satanic pacts, in Jesus' name.

9. As information emerges, it may become evident that the person receiving treatment needs to take some type of personal action, and when this happens, order the demon to terminate the manifestation, relinquish control and return it to the person. This could involve, for example, the need to confess a sin or forgive someone.

10. Pray for God to set the person free.

11. Praise God and sing spiritual songs.

12. Read Bible passages about the power of Christians to cast out demons and Christ's victory over Satan, certain Psalms that cry out for the destruction of the enemy, and texts making reference to the specific type of demon being removed. For example, you could subject a demon of nervousness to passages about peace, or a demon of vice to passages about self-control and caring for the body as temple of the Holy Spirit.

13. Pray and rebuke in tongues, especially if the demon is speaking in satanic tongues.

14. Lay hands on the demonized person if God so directs, allowing your hands to serve as a

channel of God's power. Demons sometimes respond to this touch by screaming, "You're burning me!" clearly indicating that God's power is at work.

15. Ask God to:

   a. Reveal any information necessary to complete the deliverance.
   b. Release any repressed or forgotten memories that may be harming the person.
   c. Break any blockages the demons may have set up to interfere with the deliverance.

16. Command the demon to depart from the person and send it to the Abyss or to Jesus.

17. Ask the Holy Spirit to take control of all areas being released as the demons leave.

18. Continue following this same sequence of steps until all demons are gone. Sometimes the whole process can be completed in a single session, while other cases may require many sessions.

19. Follow-up support is needed to see that the person is maturing psychologically and spiritually after deliverance, because the demons will be looking for any openings to re-enter.

DEMONIC MANIFESTATION

Sometimes a demon shows up entirely unprovoked, often during a religious service when the power of God is quite noticeable, or in the presence of someone who is particularly full of the Spirit of God. This happened in the Bible story of the demon-possessed Gadarene who shouted out at Jesus when he approached. The demons inside the man could not tolerate being so close to the spiritual power they sensed in Jesus and begged him to leave them alone.

Other times demons stay in hiding and do not manifest spontaneously but need to be confronted verbally and forced into view. "Manifesting" in this context means a demon emerges from its hiding place inside the person, taking total or partial control and producing bodily motions or speech, whether using the sufferer's voice or an unfamiliar voice. It may even produce animal-like sounds or speak in a language unknown to its victim.

A person under demonic influence may display a wide variety of behaviors, including:

1. Convulsions

2. Trembling

3. A feeling of pressure in the head or chest

4. A sensation similar to a rubber band squeezing the head or other part of the body

5. Rapid eye movements (R.E.M.)

6. Cold or chills

7. Pain

8. Weeping

9. Fear

10. Screaming

11. Strange noises

12. Sighing, moaning

13. Blasphemy or curses against God or the deliverance minister

14. Uncontrollable laughter

15. Jeering laughter

16. Rage, fury

17. Insults, threats

18. Destructive impulses

19. Pleading not to be cast out

20. Requesting permission to enter someone else

21. Restlessness

22. Anxiety, distress

23. Despair

24. Desire to flee

25. Nausea

26. Strange languages

27. Speaking in human languages unknown to the person

28. Disturbing mental images

29. Attempts to distract

30. Constant singing or talking to block the voice of the deliverance minister

31. Attempting to bargain with the deliverance minister, offering power or riches

32. Strange sensations

Allowing the spirit to speak

This is a very controversial topic. Many ministers order the demon to leave quietly to protect the person being delivered, or in the belief that anything the demon says will be a lie anyway. Others rely on their gift of revelation, trusting that God will reveal whatever they need to know and obviating any need for the demons to talk.

In my practice I prefer to order demons to manifest. I have found that patients themselves benefit from the physical and verbal manifestation because it helps them to understand and deeply believe that the attack is from actual demons and not a mere consequence of suggestion or hysteria.

Moreover, a demon may disclose information that reveals useful facts, such as what type of demon it is, what parts of the person's life are under its dominion, how it got in, whether certain spiritual doors should be shut to prevent the demon from returning, whether the person has experienced unconscious trauma or is harboring unforgiveness against someone else, whether the person has been targeted by witchcraft that needs to be broken, and so forth. Sometimes the deliverance can be completed without this information, but not always. A demon may refuse to leave unless its foothold has been revealed and addressed, which can be done easily if the demon is forced to confess what it knows.

I agree that it may not always be necessary for the demon to talk, but I still find it very helpful because the demon often supplies information applicable in the patient's on-going treatment and useful for prevention. If the demon says, for example, that it entered through a Ouija board, the person learns that this seemingly innocent game of the occult can be dangerous and should be avoided in the future. The patient may also caution others against such practices. The message seems to be much more effective if the person hears it directly from the demon rather than from the minister.

TOUCHING A DEMON-POSSESSED PERSON

Some ministers avoid any physical contact with the person who is in deliverance, in the belief that demons could pass into them or hurt them in some way. It seems to me that anyone who is afraid that a demon might pass in should stay away from deliverance ministry altogether, because the fear itself makes them vulnerable. The demon could seize on the fear to press an attack. This happened to me the very first time I was alone during a demonic manifestation, but I had to quickly overcome this fear standing firmly on God's Word. Otherwise, I never could have continued in deliverance ministry.

Sometimes I use physical touch, and sometimes I refrain. I have often felt God's leading to stand and place my hands over some part of the person's body, and the results have convinced me it was truly of God. The demons often begin to howl at the very first touch, shouting, "Don't touch me!" "You're burning me." "There is fire in your hands." "Get your hands off me." "Ouch, it hurts." Other times the deliverance is activated the instant I make physical contact, as the patient begins to vomit or burp. It seems a clear sign that God can use a Christian's hands as the channel of his healing and delivering power.

I have seen many cases of particularly violent manifestations brought under control by binding the demon verbally and ordering it to keep still in Jesus' name, but in a few cases, this is not enough. For example, I have seen demons that attempt to attack my client by causing him to scratch himself with his own hands, bang his head on the floor, pummel his legs with his own fists, bite his lips of his tongue, clamp his jaws together powerfully or grind his teeth hard enough to fracture them, wrap his hands around his own throat to strangle himself, and other similar reactions.

There is no question that such patients need to be physically restrained by gripping their hands or grasping their heads to prevent them from hurting themselves, because the demon must not be allowed to physically harm its victim. Sometimes I need to bring in reinforcements to help me restrain the person. I have seen only a few cases where real harm was done:

1. One woman broke off a piece of her tooth when the demons caused her to clamp her jaws together violently.

2. On another occasion, after a demon entered a woman's eyes and attempted to stare me down with chilling expressions, her eyes became seriously bloodshot.

3. Scratches and bruises.

They have never done me any harm, despite their many threats. They have tried to kick me, scratch me, strangle me and throw things at me, but in such cases I simply command the demon to release the person's hands or legs, and an invisible power forces it to obey. They have never done anything worse than spit at me. God's protection becomes palpably evident as he infuses his children with his own authority.

Some of my clients have occasionally become so violent that we need to push the furniture out of the way and let them flail around on the floor until the demons are worn out. These patients end up exhausted, bruised and sore, but sometimes it cannot be avoided. Try to provide patients with a soft, sturdy armchair to protect them from harm if the demon produces physical blows or movements so violent as to collapse a more rickety chair. A carpeted room may also be best for such situations.

I would strongly discourage physical contact ministering to a person of the opposite sex who is under a spirit of lust, or a person of the same sex under a homosexual spirit, as such demons can take advantage of physical contact to cause sexual arousal in the patient. Also, if the demon is violent, do not enter into a physical struggle with it, unless it absolutely doesn't respond to the command of releasing you.

Another serious mistake, which unfortunately I have observed, is to place your hands on the patient's erogenous zones, especially patients of the opposite sex or homosexuals of the same sex. If you as minister are ever truly convinced that the spirit has a foothold in these zones and hands must be laid on them, place the client's own hand over the area, and then, if absolutely necessary, place your hand over the patient's hand. If the manifestation is too strong for the patient to cooperate this way, have someone of the same sex lay on hands, and never anyone of the opposite sex, if the person is heterosexual.

HOW THE DEMON LEAVES

Demons often exit via a bodily process: vomit, tears, sweat, tremors, snorts, belches from the mouth or nose, screams, loud howls of laughter, hemorrhage, urine, forceful abdominal contractions, sneezes, coughs, yawns, air escaping through the ears. The person may feel a physical sensation when it leaves and suddenly say, "It's gone. I felt it leave."

Sometimes the spirit itself speaks and says, "I'm leaving," which may or may not be true because it could have actually found somewhere else to hide inside the person. Conversely, there may be no visible sign that the spirit has gone, but the symptoms vanish, constituting clear proof that the spirit is no longer present.

Some people, who have a special gift of seeing demons, can identify where they are located in the affected person and can tell when they are hiding. When certain demons refuse to manifest, it can be very useful to have such a person present to use this gift or some other gift of revelation so God can show what is in the person and whether it has left.

FILLING THE HOUSE

Once the evil spirit has left, ask God to send his Holy Spirit to fill the empty space left behind and prevent the demons from returning. The Bible says in Luke 11:24-26, "*When an impure spirit comes out of a person, it goes through arid places seeking rest and does not find it. Then it says, 'I will return to the house I left.' When it arrives, it finds the house swept clean and put in order. Then it goes and takes seven other spirits more wicked than itself, and they go in and live there. And the final condition of that person is worse than the first."*

This is a clear call to preventive action. People who have completed deliverance must invest time in spiritual growth and be filled with God as much as they can so if any spirit tries to return, it will find the house is not empty, but full of God's presence.

BARRIERS TO DELIVERANCE

Demons generally have a foothold, something within the person that the demon can grasp onto and gain control over a certain area of the person's life: unconfessed sin, failure to forgive, psychological trauma, or even witchcraft committed against the person. The only way to break the demon's grip is to address every foothold, because otherwise, when the demon is ordered to leave, it may either refuse to go at all or else slip away and then return.

If the foothold is sin, it must be confessed to God to receive forgiveness. In the case of emotional trauma, you can ask God to send his power and grant inner healing. Psychotherapy or counseling may be the best way of alerting the person's conscious mind to the source of problems, while in other cases, God reveals the roots through prayer and heals them directly.

Resentment and unforgiveness need to be confronted head-on, because if we ourselves refuse to forgive, neither will God forgive, heal or deliver. Once when I ordered a demon to leave during a deliverance session, it answered, "I don't have to, because he has refused to forgive so-and-so for some offense or other." I ordered it to relinquish its control over the man's voice and asked whether the demon's claim was true. He agreed that it was, so I walked him through forgiveness.

When I ordered the demon to speak again, it grumbled, "That was a dirty trick!"

"So now you have to go, right?" I asked.

"Yes," it replied.

"Then go now," I ordered. The demon left without another word, its foothold severed.

THE OCCULT

All witchcraft and spells need to be broken and canceled in Jesus' name. People are not always aware that they have been subject to witchcraft, but the demons can disclose who sent them and what type of spell was cast. God's revelation always comes into play, because if the demons refuse to talk, or even if they do explain it themselves, you still need to ask God to reveal the truth and confirm the unclean spirit's claims.

People who are themselves involved in the occult need to renounce all such practices, but this alone is not enough. Demonic invasion sometimes persists even after the sufferer has renounced and confessed this kind of sin, because a variety of spirits may have entered through occult practices and need to be specifically confronted and cast out in Jesus' name.

Even victims who have never taken part in occult practices may have friends or relatives who have. Such well-intentioned friends sometimes try to "help," in the only way they know how, to attract a boyfriend, get a husband to stop drinking, find a job, or be healed or delivered, and all this needs to be broken in Jesus' name.

Other people may have sought help from a practitioner of witchcraft because they realized they are in some type of spiritual bondage. They mistakenly believe that one witch can undo spells cast by another, and they end up even more demonized than they were before. They may feel better or find what they were looking for, but none of this is free; the devil will collect his due in the end, and the person will not even realize it.

The Bible is clear about this, all the way back to Deuteronomy 18:9-15, when God warns his people not to adopt the occult practices of the heathens:

> When you enter the land the Lord your God
> is giving you, do not learn to imitate the
> detestable ways of the nations there. Let no
> one be found among you who sacrifices their
> son or daughter in the fire, who practices
> divination or sorcery, interprets omens,
> engages in witchcraft, or casts spells, or who
> is a medium or spiritist or who consults
> the dead. Anyone who does these things is
> detestable to the Lord; because of these same
> detestable practices the Lord your God will
> drive out those nations before you. You must
> be blameless before the Lord your God. The
> nations you will dispossess listen to those
> who practice sorcery or divination. But as
> for you, the Lord your God has not permitted
> you to do so. The Lord your God will raise up
> for you a prophet like me from among you,
> from your fellow Israelites. You must listen
> to him.

Jesus says in Luke 11:14-23 that it is impossible to cast out an evil spirit by means of another evil spirit. Such a practice is a lie, which is unfortunate because many witches and sorcerers are well-intentioned, convinced that their work is led by a power of goodness, or even by God himself. They believe that they are doing good, and far from being a sin, it is what they call "white magic." They have fallen into Satan's snares, because God condemns all witchcraft, magic, divination and sorcery. These things are all under Satan's control, disguised as the angel of light, Lucifer, to deceive many people. Jesus prescribes only one way to expel these spirits:

> ... *In my name they will drive out demons* ... (Mk 16:17), and he explains why. *When a strong man, fully armed, guards his own house, his possessions are safe. But when someone stronger attacks and overpowers him, he takes away the armor in which the man trusted and divides up his plunder. Whoever is not with me is against me, and whoever does not gather with me, scatters* (Lk 11:21-23).

The "house" in this parable is the person afflicted by demons, and the "strong man," the demon, defends it until someone stronger, Jesus, comes and seizes control of the house. Those who try to take control using any other power that is not in Jesus' name push people toward perdition instead of gathering them to God.

Occult practitioners generally have spiritual gifts and a desire to help, but no one has taught them to use these gifts correctly. They could stay out of this trap and avoid being used by demons if their churches helped them identify their gifts, understand them and develop them under God's leading.

People involved in occult practices are actually misusing their God-given gifts in the service of the devil. Satan and his legions happily take over peoples' gifts to serve their own interests, and they do it by identifying those who have especially powerful gifts and luring them into occult practices.

For example, a person endowed by God with a gift of prophecy may fall under the wiles of a spirit of divination, and when the spirit is eventually expelled, the gift still remains and is now free to function as it was meant to, under the control of the Holy Spirit. Anyone who understands this fully will find it easy to give up the practice of divination.

The same is true for people who have the gift of healing. Even after they are free of the demon's harmful influence and no longer honor Satan through their cures, they can still wield their gift, but now for the glory of God.

People who have God's gift of vision and are involved in the occult will see satanic visions. Some who have the gift of tongues and are tangled up with demons will speak satanic tongues. If they have the gift of revelation, they will place it at the service of demons. After people have been delivered in Jesus' name, their spiritual gifts begin to operate freely, under Gods' control.

SPIRITUAL INHERITANCE

People are sometimes faced with another type of foothold not of their own making—a spiritual inheritance from past generations. It is a condition familiar to psychology because of the strength of parental modeling, meaning that a parent's mistakes are instinctively replicated by their children and future generations until someone finally stands up to this inheritance and defeats it.

The fact is that current generations are paying the price for actions their ancestors may have taken contrary to God's will, and the only one who can put a stop to it is God himself. The generational law can be lifted if we draw near to God, enter into a new covenant with him, ask him to cancel punishments inflicted for the sins of our ancestors and expel any demons that may have entered our lives through this inheritance. So we pray for God to cut off all negative spiritual inheritance and replace it with the inheritance of the same heavenly father who promises to "... [show] love to a thousand generations of those who love me and keep my commandments" (Ex 20:6).

SUSCEPTIBILITY TO DEMONIC INFLUENCE

When I first started looking into the demonic, I visited other groups, both Roman Catholic and Protestant, that were practicing spiritual deliverance. I found that they did not give a thought to psychology, but concentrated exclusively on getting rid of the demon. I could not help but observe a clear relationship between the types of demons affecting the persons being ministered and their own psychological traumas and profiles, and I was particularly surprised to see them reliving past trauma during deliverance sessions.

I have since looked much more deeply into the events that occur during spiritual deliverance, and I have realized that specific demons do not go after just any person chosen at random. It is no coincidence that a given demon attacks one person instead of another, because an underlying trauma or specific weakness makes the chosen target susceptible to the influence of this particular demon.

A demon of homosexuality, for example, goes after someone whose family background or sexual development creates a special vulnerability to homosexual patterns of behavior. I am not suggesting all homosexuals are under demonic influence, and although it has been true for those I have treated, and I hesitate to generalize, I am inclined to think it is so, based on my experience.

I also know that simply casting out a demon of homosexuality will not solve the person's problem. Too many deliverance ministers have failed to understand that if the person's psychological issues are not understood and resolved, the demon is likely to return. The opposite is also true, as a homosexual under demonic influence cannot attempt to change his or her sexual identity through psychotherapy alone. An understanding of the whole psychological picture is useful but will never be enough for a full, lasting cure unless the demons are also expelled.

The same is true for the many people who suffer from alcoholism, hypochondria, obsessive-compulsive disorders, schizophrenia, depression and so many other apparently psychological conditions.

More puzzling still, it seems that people do not necessarily require a specific process of spiritual deliverance to be freed of demonic influence. My experience tells me that God, in his sovereignty, directly delivers many people when they simply ask for it or when others intercede for them.

I believe that people are not instantly freed of all the demons in their lives when they give their lives to God or when others pray for them. Some do flee at that moment, but he seems to leave others in place and teaches us to fight them ourselves and, in the process, learn to wage spiritual warfare. These spiritual confrontations are the best way for us to grow stronger and learn to use God's power.

God decides which demons to take out of our lives effortlessly, and which ones need to be fought, because only he knows our capacity to withstand. This is part of the promise given in 1 Corinthians 10:13, that God will not let us be tempted beyond what we can bear, and when we are tempted, he will also provide a way out.

Psychotherapy, inner healing and deliverance

I once treated a pastor who seemed a clear example of this principle. He had been an alcoholic before coming to faith, and although God had set him free almost effortlessly, he still struggled intensely with smoking. He was a counselor with years of experience, but despite it all, his own problem stubbornly persisted, undermining his reputation as a pastor and even his self-image. He would sneak off to smoke in secret, wracked with feelings of guilt.

I asked him if he might be open to the possibility of a demon lying at the root of this vice, and he replied that although he had never considered it, he was willing to receive anything coming from God that would help him stop smoking. We asked for discernment, and God confirmed that yes, there were demons in his life. God added, however, that before we could expel the demons, this pastor needed inner healing from psychological traumas that were giving the spirits a foothold. My assistant and I began to pray for him, and God put him through three regressions re-living particular situations from his past, and then healed his wounds.

The first was when he was born. As we ministered, he began to cry like a baby, whimpering, "Mama, please don't leave me. I want my mother." I placed my arm on his chest, and he seized it and gripped it with all his strength. My assistant placed her hands on his head. God used this human touch to heal a memory, and as he returned to a moment in his past, he re-experienced a time when he was a baby, desperate for the warmth of his mother's body, and suddenly felt that he had finally obtained what he was longing for.

The pastor later told us his mother had not breast-fed him, but that during this healing experience he had felt his mothers' breast, as if she had been nursing him. This was the psychological root of his oral craving, which he unconsciously tried to satisfy with cigarettes, and it came to the surface when we ordered the demon to reveal its foothold. We then commanded the demon to cease its repression of this memory and release it into the conscious mind, where God healed the old wound.

When we ordered the spirits to reveal other footholds, the second trauma arose. My assistant saw a vision and told us, "I am seeing a sad, lonely teenager." The words were no sooner out of her mouth than the pastor broke down and cried bitterly, moaning, "That's exactly how I felt when I was a teenager–alone, insecure and depressed, and now all those feelings are back." When I prayed for healing, God took away the negative feelings as tears rolled down his cheeks.

By the time we got to the third regression, the demon's manifestation had become fully evident, so I addressed it directly and said, "Who are you?"

"Rage!" it snarled.

"I want to see it," I replied.

"It's very ugly," the demon told me, "and you won't like it."

"Go ahead and show me," I said. "I am not afraid."

"I want to take a knife and kill you," it roared.

I asked God to heal this memory and free him from the anger he had once felt, and the pastor then told us his story. Years earlier, his brother, who was seriously ill at the time, had done something that infuriated him, but he knew he could not hit someone who was sick. He was so angry that he could not contain himself, so he picked up a knife and threw it wildly at his brother, who fortunately was struck by the handle rather than the blade.

He was terrified by what he had done and began to live in fear of his rage, never knowing whether he might lose his temper again and really hurt someone. He had never again allowed himself to express anger, preferring to repress it. God healed him so that he would no longer need to swallow his bad feelings, as this repressed fury had provided fertile ground for the demon of rage.

The deliverance session could not proceed, and we could not confront the demons directly, without first seeking inner healing. Three demons were working together to drive this man to cigarettes: insecurity, anxiety and vice. Their first words were spoken to my assistant in her mind, which was her particular type of spiritual gift.

"We don't want to go," they said. "We interfere with his ministry by making him smoke, and if we go, God will start to use him powerfully, even in spiritual deliverance. We need to stop him."

The demon of vice then manifested and spoke directly through the pastor's mouth, saying, "But he likes me. I give him pleasure and he enjoys it."

The pastor himself interrupted, took control and forcefully answered the demon, "I renounce your form of pleasure and I want nothing more to do with your trash in my body. My true pleasure comes from all that God gives, but yours is fake, it's a lie. I choose to keep what God gives me and I reject you."

After he spoke these words, the pastor appeared infused with visible strength. He stood up, walked over to his briefcase, took out his cigarettes and cried out, "This is so hard!" Then he shredded the cigarettes with his hands, flung them violently to the floor, stomped on them furiously, and finally burst out laughing. "I feel free!" he cried out. "I have never managed to do this before! I smoked for 35 years and this is the first time I've been able to destroy my own cigarettes. Praise be to God and thank you, Jesus Christ!"

God then led us to take authority over all symptoms of substance withdrawal that might affect him after cessation of smoking. We also spoke to his body in Jesus' name, informing it that it would no longer need tobacco because God would supply its needs. Finally, God told us we should continue to pray for him for four days and fast on the fourth day, which we did. He never smoked from that moment forward and told us that the only discomfort he experienced in the next few days was mild stomach pain.

This is a clear illustration of a persistent behavior problem resolved very quickly in a treatment combining psychological healing with prayer and the confrontation of spiritual forces in Jesus' name. I have seen similar outcomes in many cases involving multiple symptoms, which is why I am convinced that people who minister spiritual deliverance need to develop a clear understanding of the psychological processes affecting the people they minister. My recommendation, to obtain optimum results, is to combine spiritual deliverance with inner healing and psychotherapy, as all these fields are so closely interwoven.

CHAPTER 15

PRACTICAL SUGGESTIONS FOR MINISTERING DELIVERANCE

TAKE CARE OF YOUR OWN PERSONAL LIFE

1. Make sure you are in good standing in your relationship with God and with others. Satan knows people very well, and you can never outwit him in this.

   Remember the case of the Jewish exorcists who, while not followers of Christ, tried to cast out demons in Jesus' name, saying, *"'In the name of Jesus, whom Paul preaches, I command you to come out' ... the evil spirit answered them, 'Jesus I know, and Paul I know about, but who are you?' Then the man who had the evil spirit jumped on them and overpowered them all. He gave them such a beating that they ran out of the house naked and bleeding"* (Ac 19:13-16). This example is not intended to scare anyone away from deliverance ministry but should simply remind us all that that demons know Jesus and know who truly belongs to him and who does not. They may also be aware of your sins, which is why you must confess them before beginning to minister, with the assurance of God's promised forgiveness.

Despite these precautions, if a demon should rise up in the midst of battle and launch an attack because of some unconfessed sin, all you need to do is confess it immediately and receive God's forgiveness. *"If we confess our sins, he is faithful and just and will forgive us our sins and purify us from all unrighteousness"* (I Jn 1:9). Then you reply, "God has forgiven me and your accusations are worthless."

A demon may also try to fling false accusations at you, especially in team ministry when you work with other people, to embarrass you in front of them. Simply bind its lying tongue and force it to speak only the truth.

2. If you want to minister in this area, you should also prepare by going through your own inner healing and deliverance. You will not become immune to all future temptations or

conflicts, but at least you will be equipped to handle them correctly.

3. I am convinced that all believers, especially those who minister deliverance, must have people covering them and supporting them in prayer. You also need to keep yourself healthy and have a trusted counselor so you can air your own personal problems on a regular basis.

God gave me a specific message on this subject in 1985, to share with my church family: "Let none of the faithful who minister to others be expected to minister to themselves as well and bear their own burdens alone. You must uphold one another. You who minister physical healing, take care of those who minister deliverance, so that all my people both give and receive ministry. Let none of my ministers be prideful, but humbly and thankfully accept the ministrations of others. This is how my church must function, where all minister and all receive ministry, together in harmony, serving and being served, so that everyone's needs are met and everyone helps bear the weight."

This is especially crucial for those who minister deliverance, because they quickly become the target of multiple spiritual attacks intended to drive them out of the fight. These attacks are nothing to fear, as Jesus himself warned when he urged us onward: *"I have told you these things, so that in me you may have peace. In this world you will have trouble. But take heart! I have overcome the world"* (Jn 16:33).

4. Please do not misunderstand my recommendation about setting your personal life in order. It would be easy to delay the work he has set out for you, waiting until your life is perfect, but the upshot is that you will never start at all. The Bible says, *"... he who began a good work in you will carry it on to completion until the day of Christ Jesus"* (Php 1:6). This means that the Holy Spirit works continually to transform and perfect us in a lifelong process that unfolds even as God uses us to help others.

5. God may lead you to fast as a part of your personal preparation for spiritual confrontation. A passage in Mark 9:29 shows us a frustrated crew of disciples unable to deliver a boy with a demon. Jesus rebukes the evil spirit, it comes out, and the boy is healed. He then chides his disciples for failing at the task, commenting that they had too little faith and that *"This kind can come out only by prayer and fasting."*

I myself have confronted demons of this kind. I once ministered deliverance to a woman who had served as a medium and had been very sick for years. Twice I challenged the demon to no avail, and it did not even manifest. I asked God to show me how to break the power of this spirit, and he instructed me to take a three-day fast: on day one, I was to eat only fruits and vegetables, day two, only water, and day three, fruits and vegetables. He ordered the fast for all three of us – the two who were ministering, and the woman being delivered. We met for a third attempt after we had scrupulously followed his instructions, and the demon manifested violently and left.

ALWAYS TAKE THE BROAD VIEW

If you want to get involved in this ministry of deliverance, you should have some knowledge of psychology and, if possible, the rudiments of medicine to avoid narrowly attributing every problem or symptom to demons and nothing but demons.

As human beings, we are made up of body, soul and spirit, all blended into a single unit, and diagnosis can be very difficult because whatever affects one dimension affects them all. The symptoms of a brain tumor could easily be mistaken for a psychological ailment, while at the same time, a true conversion disorder, whose sufferer suddenly becomes paralyzed or blind, could be wrongly identified as an organic problem. A convulsive crisis does not necessarily mean epilepsy, but could be caused by a high degree of stress and anxiety, or instead, by a demon. Foaming at the mouth may be evidence of a departing demon, but it could also reveal a case of epilepsy or rabies. Depression may actually be a physical problem, the result of exhaustion, overwork, sleeplessness and no free time.

Deafness may be neither organic nor psychological, but spiritual, or it could even be all three at once. For example, the ear may have experienced physical damage, a psychological problem could cause the person to avoid hearing certain unpleasant sounds in the environment, and both could come together with a spirit of deafness. Treatment of only one of these dimensions will probably fail to restore the person's hearing.

God can reveal the full diagnosis and the best treatment option if you can only be sensitive to his voice. God has often directed me in ministry to lay on hands for physical healing of some affected part of the subject's body, while at the same time to be praying for inner healing from a particularly traumatic past experience. Again, human beings are a single complex package, and a full solution can be achieved only if you cultivate as many gifts and types of knowledge as possible. This way you can be prepared to tackle problems in any of the three human dimensions.

People who come to you for help may in fact need deliverance, but what they need even more is to be heard, to be given the opportunity to unburden themselves with someone who understands. They need to be fed, to grow spiritually by learning the Word of God.

They may be facing an important decision, such as a change of job, leaving their parents' home, starting school, joining a church, developing a nascent artistic talent, undertaking a physical fitness program, or adopting a healthier diet. Many diverse factors come into play for a person to enjoy the abundant life that Christ has promised.

Your work as a counselor or minister is to help them discover and identify the "thief" that is stealing, killing and destroying (Jn 10:10). It may be an evil spirit, but it could perfectly well be poor time management, stress over a looming difficult situation, or even a physical illness. If you discover problems that surpass your own ability to address as minister, suggest that the person go to a doctor, a psychologist or some other professional trained to help.

Always remember, though, that the person is a single, multidimensional being who needs to be treated as such and not simply divided up into segments so the minister treats the spirit, the physician the body and the psychologist the soul. All aspects of each area interact with one another and need to be understood as such. For example, a young man who comes down with hepatitis on his wedding day could very well become depressed and angry with God for allowing such a thing to happen, and needs attention to all three dimensions in order to be fully healed.

I happen to believe that the spiritual dimension is uppermost because the entire being can often by healed by addressing spiritual issues. Never forget, therefore, that God may want to use you as a channel for the whole process. If God instructs you to lay hands on the person and let his healing power flow though them, just do it! If he shows you to pray for healing of memories, just do it! If he also tells you to expel a demon, just do it! God will be glorified in a wonderful way through that person if you simply follow his leading.

CHAPTER 16

CHRISTIANS WITH DEMONS?

I was always taught that no true Christian could come under demonic invasion because an unclean spirit can never occupy the same body as the Holy Spirit. I knew the scriptural backing for this doctrine, as for example,

> You, dear children, are from God and have overcome them, because the one who is in you is greater than the one who is in the world" (1 Jn 4:4).

> Do not be yoked together with unbelievers. For what do righteousness and wickedness have in common? Or what fellowship can light have with darkness? What harmony is there between Christ and Belial? Or what does a believer have in common with an unbeliever? What agreement is there between the temple of God and idols? For we are the temple of the living God (2 Co 6:14-16).

This belief colored my whole world view, and I felt secure in my Christian invulnerability, until I decided to look more deeply into the field of demonic deliverance. As a psychologist and a believer, I began to have direct experiences with unclean spirits and hear demons talk to me through the mouths of Christian clients. This put me into a tailspin as my confidently held beliefs began to crumble.

"Lord," I protested, "this is not supposed to happen! What about my theology? No demon can speak through the mouth of a Christian. Or can it? How can this be happening right in front of me?"

I tried to come up with answers. "Maybe these are not demons," I said to myself, "but clinical cases, multiple personalities." But why would I be coming across so many instances of dissociative identity disorder when the psychology literature has barely enough of these extremely rare cases to even report them? And why do these personalities start to appear whenever I bind demons and order them to speak, in Jesus' name? Why do they speak out in rejection of Christ or anything having to do with God, and why so much hatred of the people standing up to them? Why do they call themselves "spirits?"

I pressed on, looking for answers. Maybe these people, deep down, are just pretending to be believers and aren't Christians at all. But shouldn't I be able to distinguish a Christian from a non-Christian? Why do I feel that the Holy Spirit is testifying to my spirit that these people are true believers, and why do I know in my spirit that it's true?

I began looking through Christian literature, searching out definitions of the term "Christian," but the more I read, the more I felt convinced in my heart that I could not claim these people were somehow less than Christian.

Something else happened which further cleared up any doubts about demonic influence in Christians and convinced me even more that Christians can, in fact, come under attack.[4] A close acquaintance, a Christian colleague, once came to me and said, "I think I need deliverance."

"What are you talking about?" I objected, "What do you mean, you need deliverance? You, a mature Christian, a psychologist, who has been through professional training, therapy and inner healing? I would think you, of all people, would be able to take care of anything demonic yourself," I said.

"No!" she pleaded. "I have been struggling with these things for years now. I tried prayer, fasting and

---

4   DEMONIC INFLUENCE: Partial interference with some facet of the person, exercised though the mind. While a demon CANNOT force Christians to do or say anything against their will, if it has accrued enough influence over the mind, the temptation may be too strong to withstand without help. Affected persons may need to ask for help from another believer who has developed more robust spiritual authority, to wage the battle for them until such time as they are able to build up their spiritual muscle and can fight for themselves to gain full control of their own actions. Certain areas can become vulnerable to demonic influence if they are weakened by psychological or spiritual factors.

counseling, but nothing has worked. You see, I am a compulsive liar. I tell the stupidest, most unnecessary lies you can imagine. I'm a Christian, I know that lying is wrong, I don't want to lie, and still I catch myself telling lies all the time. I don't know why I do it, I don't know why I can't seem to stop, and I'm convinced there has to be a demon behind it.

"There's something else. Whenever I start to sense that God is telling me to do something, I feel a powerful drive to do just the opposite, like Jonah. I love God, I want to do his will and I want to obey him in everything. I have told him I'm willing to do whatever he wants me to, but something inside wants me not to. I think it's a demon, I need deliverance and I want you to minister it to me. I have been following your work in this field, I have seen that you know what you're doing and that's why I'm here."

I silently wished I were half so sure of myself as she was and that I actually knew what I was doing. I reluctantly set an appointment for her, willing to help but honestly doubting that anything would happen. The session began, and I started by telling her that I would pray and rebuke whatever she felt needed rebuking, but that I didn't expect any manifestations.

"Look, Rita," she said, "last night when I prayed about this session, God spoke to me and said that if I would be completely open with you and hide nothing, he would set me free today. So I don't care if there is a manifestation, and if the demons have to talk before we can get them out, so be it. I don't much care for the idea of a manifestation, but if it comes, it comes."

I began as I usually do, praying for God to protect us, our families and our material possessions. Then I bound the evil spirits, broke Satan's power over her life and began to rebuke the lying spirit that she had discerned. I selected several Bible passages against lying and read them aloud, but I held back from ordering the demon to manifest because I did not want to embarrass myself in front of my colleague if nothing happened.

Suddenly, a strange noise issued from her mouth. She was stuttering. I listened and then asked, "Is this your prayer language, your tongues?"

"No," she said, "something strange is happening to my mouth. This is not my speaking in tongues, it's completely different."

That was all I needed to muster up the courage and command the lying demon to manifest and tell me what other demons were in there. The stuttering was coming so loud and fast that I could not make out what it was saying until I suddenly realized that the sounds were not simply noise, but real syllables. They were pouring forth at such an astonishing speed that it was impossible to make out the words.

"Stop stuttering and speak clearly," I demanded.

The stuttering slowed enough that I could finally make out the word, "Doubt, doubt, doubt."

"Are you a spirit of doubt?" I asked.

"Yes, yes, yes, yes," came the reply, fast and furious.

"Is a spirit pushing her to run away from God's calling?" I asked.

"Yes, yes, yes, yes," rattled the stuttering voice.

"Who else is there?" I asked.

"Pain, pain, pain," it hammered.

"Emotional pain?"

"Yes, yes, yes, yes."

I asked the demon of pain whether some past experience needed to be healed, but it answered "no." It said that God had already healed the painful memories, but this spirit was retaining the pain itself.

The session continued until we had identified twelve demons, and they all spoke through the mouth of my Christian colleague. She would start puffing and panting every time I ordered a demon to leave, blowing air out through her mouth, and every time she stopped puffing, I asked the remaining demons if the previous one was gone. If they said it was, I proceeded to cast out the next one. Occasionally the voice told me it wasn't completely out, so I again ordered it to go until all the remaining demons, which I had bound to truth, told me it was gone.

When the last one fled and my colleague opened her eyes, I asked her whether she had been able to recognize each demon's sphere of influence in her life. She said she had been surprised to hear some of the names, and she had never guessed there were so many. Even so, each time they identified themselves, she suddenly realized that those particular areas of her life were indeed problems for her, and although she had not been aware of it until that moment, she could confirm their presence.

A year has gone by since her deliverance session, and my friend continues to be free of these problem areas. She has given her testimony to several Christian groups because she wants other believers to know that they, too, may be needing spiritual deliverance from demonic forces, just as she did.

A few days after my colleague's spiritual victory, I received another client, a woman who had experienced demon-related physical symptoms. The demon was speaking very fluently, so I took the opportunity to ask it a question that had been troubling me.

"You," I said, "are an unclean spirit, so how can you be living inside a Christian and speaking through her mouth?"

"I am in her mind," it answered.

"And what about her body?"

"No, I can't get into her body because there's something else living there."

"You mean the Holy Spirit?"

"Yes, you know him too."

"But then how can you make her body sick?"

"I do it through her mind, because if I can get into her mind I can control her body."

I didn't want to turn the session into a séance instead of a deliverance, so I decided to cut the conversation short and cast out the demon. Theology should not be built on what demons have to say, which could lead into dangerous territory, but it seemed to me that this demon was telling the truth.

I have seen too many other cases where the same thing seemed to be happening. Over a span of many years, I have heard demons talk to me through the mouths of hundreds of true Christians. Four of them, evangelical pastors from non-Pentecostal denominations. They found themselves hard pressed to accept the idea that they had demons, but once they decided to undergo spiritual deliverance, they ended up completely symptom-free.

I have also witnessed non-verbal demonic manifestations in hundreds of other Christian believers. A number of people working in spiritual warfare join me as eyewitnesses, and as I cannot discount so much evidence, I have been forced to rethink the conventional evangelical belief that no Christian can be demonized.

I do believe it is impossible for a Christian to be **possessed** per se, because a person in such a state would be under the full domination of a demon.[5] Christians are always under the rule of the Holy Spirit, at least in broad areas that no demon can ever occupy. There are, however, other areas in the lives of many Christians that

5   DEMON POSSESSION: Mastery over human will by demons. Possessed people, despite every desire to the contrary, are unable to stop obeying the demands of controlling spirits. They may not even be cognizant that they are being used by demons. They can be forced to say or do things against their own will, even in a state of unconsciousness, and the demons can take over full control of their minds and bodies so that victims have no memory of what they have said or done. A Christian CANNOT be possessed, but CAN come under demonic influence.
1.   Untreated emotional trauma or scars
2.   Parts of the personality or will that have not been fully surrendered to God
3.   Spiritually inherited bondage from ancestors for unconfessed sin or satanic pacts
4.   Contamination from contact with occult practices
5.   Contamination due to nagging awareness of a sin
6.   Contamination of the five senses through pornography, satanic music, satanic toys and games, horror films or material containing teachings contrary to Scripture.

can be under demonic influence, whether by inheritance, involvement in the occult, witchcraft or curses spoken against them, unconfessed sin or unforgiveness of another person, or trauma, and my experience tells me that this influence needs to be cut off and cast out.

If my interpretation of these events is correct, Christian psychologists and counselors are standing at the forefront of a whole new field of research. We are trained to work with a person's mind and emotions, but maybe we should first find out if unwelcome visitors are trying to confuse and destroy our attempts to build up a person's mental health.

CHAPTER 17

WHY DO SOME DEMONS SPEAK WHILE OTHERS DO NOT?

When all of this started, God brought many people to my counseling office and made the demons in them manifest verbally. He was teaching me about the demonic realm and about how to cast a demon out of a person. He was using the demons to train me. Week after week the cases streamed in and I kept on learning.

But this question kept popping up inside me. Why do some demons speak while others do not? I asked God about this, but got no direct answer from him, until one day he presented me with a question: "What do the people experiencing a verbal demonic manifestation have in common?"

I didn't have the answer, but his words made me more observant, trying to discover the answer. Finally it donned on me! They're prophets! They have a prophetic mouth! Oh, now I understand! Only prophetic mouths are connected to the spirit realm. Only prophets have the spiritual gift, the spiritual apparatus, that allows a spiritual voice to be projected into the physical world through a physical mouth in order to be heard by physical ears.

"Right!" God answered. "Let me tell you about the prophetic channel. This term is not in the Bible but it's what I'll call it in order to explain. This spiritual apparatus, as you referred to it, is like a cell phone connecting the spirit realm to the physical realm. Anybody can pick up a cell phone and talk through it, whether it be a good person or a bad person. The cell phone is just an object that allows communication. The prophetic channel is just that, a spiritual gift that allows a spiritual voice to be heard in the physical realm."

"Obviously, I designed it and bestowed it upon those I chose to receive it in order to be able to communicate with human beings. I have always communicated with humans through a prophetic channel. I am a spirit, a Holy Spirit, and I speak to people I have gifted with spiritual hearing, but I have also created spiritual mouths through which I can speak directly, as if that mouth were my own. But if the person who has that spiritual mouth is indwelled by demons, then the demons, who are also spirits, evil spirits, can use that prophetic apparatus to communicate to the outside world. Just like a spiritual cell phone. Any spirit present can use it. It's just a means of communication between the spiritual realm and the physical realm.

"If the person being ministered does not have this prophetic channel, the demons present have no way of speaking through that mouth, even if they are present in that person. So, their deliverance is going to be different than the deliverance of the person who DOES have this prophetic gift. The demons in them are not going to manifest verbally, but you can still get them out. You confront them with my Word, using it as a sword. You break their power over the person, using the Holy Spirit's power. You use the power of truth and of praise. You use the authority I've given all believers. And the demons have to leave.

"In the case of persons who DO have a prophetic mouth, the power encounter can be verbal. You can force the demon to confess its name, its footholds, the open doors, the curses and whatever information is necessary to free that person from its bondage. Like the case of the Gadarene demoniac. Jesus commanded the demon to confess its name because he had ordered it to leave, but it was not yet obeying his command, so he demanded more information, he demanded its name. The demon confessed its name was Legion for there were many demons in this man, not just one. Knowing the demon's name gave Jesus power over it and he cast it out.

"But let me tell you something else about the prophetic channel. It's not only a means of communication, it's also a spiritual weapon. That's why I want you to know about this. I can trap a demon in the prophetic channel to force it to speak. When I want an evil spirit to reveal or confess information, I force it into the prophetic channel and I keep it in there until it says what I am commanding it to say. I want you to learn to do this. My angels can trap a demon and force it into the prophetic channel where, you, in turn, can force it to speak. The evil spirit does not like to be in there. It's uncomfortable. My angels can bring the Holy Spirit's consuming fire to torment it in there. And you have authority to keep it trapped in there until it speaks out and confesses what it's supposed to confess.

Satan has taught his servants to use the prophetic channel for his purposes, so that demons or he himself, can speak through a prophetic mouth. That's what a medium is, a person who has a prophetic mouth through which deceiving spirits can communicate with the outside world.

But now it's MY time to teach my servants about this spiritual apparatus. I do not want demons speaking whatever they want to communicate, using a prophetic mouth to deceive people. I want to force evil spirits to speak what I want them to speak and they have to obey for they are under my authority.

God brought me cases to confirm this. I was ministering to a Costa Rican woman who only spoke Spanish. The demons in her spoke to me in five different languages. They were fluent in those languages, but she wasn't. I was by myself and the deliverance session had lasted about three hours. I had not yet been able to break a particular demon's power, but I had run out of time and I needed to stop as I had other things I had to do, so I thought in my mind, "I think I'm going to have to stop here and continue this deliverance session another day." I didn't say it out loud, I only thought it. At that moment the demon said to me: "I have a message for you from your God." My reaction was: "A demon is going to give me a message from God? Yeah. Right!" To which the spirit answered: "Your God says you should not stop the confrontation because you have almost broken my power. Continue, and in five minutes you'll be able to cast me out. Obviously I did not want to say that, but he is forcing me to say it."

I was so impressed by what that demon said that I decided to believe it. I continued breaking this demon's power and commanding it to leave, and sure enough, five minutes later I was able to get it out. That definitely taught me a lesson. God is sovereign, he has all authority over the spiritual realm and demons HAVE to obey his commands. If he orders a demon to speak, like it or not, the demon has to comply.

A second opportunity to confirm this was the case of an ex-satanist I ministered in Miami. At the time, I was working in the ministry with a prophet. We had a difference of opinion regarding this topic. I had shared with him my experience with the demon who had given me God's message. He adamantly did not believe God would send a message through a demon so when we were confronting a demon in this ex-satanist woman and the demon said, "I have a message from your God," this prophet immediately blurted out: "You are lying! I'm a prophet. If God wanted to speak to us at this time, he would use MY mouth, not a demon's." To which the demon answered: "Do you think I WANT to relay your God's message? Obviously I DON'T! But he wants to show you that although we are rebellious spirits, we still have to obey his commands. This is very humiliating, but he is sovereign over us and whatever he commands we have to do. This is why I'm telling you what he is forcing me to say."

Later on, God taught me more about the use of prophets as spiritual weapons in and of themselves, but that I will reveal in another book. For now, for the purpose of this present book, it's enough to clarify that not all demons will speak in a deliverance session because not all human mouths have the gift of being able to allow a spiritual voice to speak through them, only those belonging to prophets.

CHAPTER 18

GROUNDS FOR BELIEF

I am a scientist. I believe that the scientific method was a crucial discovery of undeniable value to the progress of human knowledge. It is not the only method of obtaining information, however, because I also believe in divine revelation. Both are God-given, I accept both and am convinced that they are not only compatible, but closely interwoven.

Scientific experiments can be misinterpreted, and so can revelation from God, but in spite of it all, it is by the grace of God that human knowledge continues to advance. This is the attitude that underlies all my research into demonic activity, as I have drawn on careful study of the Bible, which I accept as the revealed Word of God, and also on scientific study of observed fact.

I have witnessed innumerable cases of people tormented or bound by demons, and I have personally confronted demons in hundreds of people. Not all deliverances have been successful, and although the majority have indeed ended in victory, I believe I have learned more from the failures than from the successes, because they push me to rethink my hypotheses and gradually improve them.

I do not claim to have discovered all there is to know about demons, nor would I ever hold my conclusions to be infallible, but I do know that they are built on conscientious, laborious fieldwork. The ideas I have expounded in this book are not mere assumptions or personal fancies, but are grounded in direct observation, formation of hypotheses, personal experimentation and development of conclusions. I have often been forced to redraft my ideas when the fieldwork confronts me with undeniable evidence.

I believe that all this research entitles me to speak out. I am on a solid footing because it is not enough to just read the Bible or other books on the subject and think you understand it all, in the absence of on-site investigation.

Why do I think this is so important? Because I am aware that I have been speaking out on a very controversial subject. I have exposed myself to criticism by psychologists, both Christian and non-Christian, who do not believe in demons. This should not come as a surprise, as many Christian psychologists feel this way.

I have also attracted the ire of theologians, ministers and lay believers convinced that it is heresy to claim that a Christian could be influenced by demons. I am perfectly aware that my thoughts on these matters will not win me any popularity contests, and I would have been better served to have just kept my mouth shut. I speak out regardless, because it pains me to see so many Christians harboring complete ignorance of all things demonic. Many refuse even to discuss the subject, whether from fear or disbelief. Others do consider it, but they have no practical experience to sustain their theoretical positions. Then there are the ones who have been through very bad experiences.

My own observations tell me that very few people have studied this field by combining the scientific method with spiritual experience. I have found that this combination can yield much more promising results, and it is what I recommend.

I have also had occasion to observe deliverances performed in ways that I cannot condone:

1. Deliverance is sometimes performed in charismatic Roman Catholic groups invoking the name of Mary instead of Jesus.

2. People may launch straight into deliverance without first taking the trouble to figure out whether a demon is in fact present.

3. Sometimes a manifestation ends and everyone relaxes, assuming the demon is gone, when in fact it is still present and has gone into hiding.

4. I have seen groups of believers gather around the person, shouting "Out, in Jesus' name!" without trying to discern what kind of demon is there, and as a result, they cannot determine afterward whether the affected area is actually free.

5. People ministering may think they are "discerning" when in fact they are projecting onto the person.

6. I have seen the process break down on the assumption that the demon has not left because the person did not vomit, as if that were the only way demons could leave.

7. The demon may have been ordered to leave screaming, and the person obediently spends hours howling and yelling, and ends up with a badly damaged throat.

8. Sometimes deliverance seems to involve hitting the person, the idea being that physical pain to the body can somehow affect the demon.

9. I have seen cases where the affected person falls to the floor, and everyone assumes deliverance is complete. This type of physical collapse may itself be a demonic manifestation, or it could be that the person is resting in the spirit. Even if it were a demonic manifestation, there is no guarantee that the unclean spirit leaves as soon as the person falls down.

Although I cannot condone any of these practices, neither do I blame the people using them. Such errors stem from the ignorance we all share regarding how to fight demons. The field of demon expulsion has been ignored in churches far too long, and the resulting taboo on discussing it means we no longer know how to do it well.

I used to be against public deliverance services because I felt that the person being ministered had a right to privacy, until one day God asked me: "Where did Jesus cast out demons, in a private room or out in the open, in front of everybody, so that people could observe God's sovereignty over demons?" To which I responded: "I get your point, Lord. OK. I'll open up to ministering deliverance in public meetings." So from then on, when I teach seminars on spiritual deliverance, I confront demons publicly. I'm still a firm believer in the individual process of deliverance which I practice in my office with my clients, but if God wants to free people in a group setting, he's the boss, and I do his bidding.

The Bible offers a great deal of assistance to anyone willing to be taught, but it is not a handbook on demon removal. It tells only a few brief stories of demonic deliverance. No one can really learn to do it until they dare to try it themselves, make mistakes and try again until they start to get it right.

It is supremely easy to criticize from afar when other people are ministering deliverance, and say, "You are doing it all wrong." Instead of criticizing, why not try to deliver someone yourself and see if it works? Or if you disagree with deliverance, why not try to heal the person some other way to see if it works?

It is very easy to say, "This person is a Christian and therefore cannot have any demons." So what can you say when a demon starts to spew blasphemy from a Christian's mouth? Or it may scream such things as, "I came into this person many years ago and I have no intention of going anywhere. Leave me alone! Who cares if Jesus is in her heart, when I am still here in her mind?"

I do not wish to offend anyone, but if the people raising these objections have never personally observed a demonic manifestation, if they have never seen a successful deliverance, if they have never interviewed a demon-affected person who has been set free, and if they have never tried to get a demon out of anyone, I cannot give weight to their opinions. I think the right to speak an opinion needs to be earned.

If your claims are not based on direct observation of the facts, in my view they are little more than prejudice, that is, casting a judgment in the absence of evidence. It remains little more than an untested hypothesis that would need to undergo an experimental process before confirming or discarding it.

Again, I am a scientist, and as such, I would challenge those who have never had direct contact with the demonic, to consider examining it scientifically. Start with a diligent study of everything the Bible has to say about it. Then seek out people and groups that are performing demon expulsion and ask how and where they do it. Visit them and request permission to be present in their sessions. Do not limit yourself to just one place, but find out how it is being done in a variety of churches, both Protestant and Roman Catholic. Then, with this practical foundation, start to develop your own theories about the demonic. Only then will you be qualified to venture an opinion. Only then will you be in a position to start testing your personal hypotheses about demons for yourself.

Gain your own practical experience with the demonic, and if you then draw conclusions different from my own, at least you have a basis for your opinion. If I am mistaken, I want to be the first to know. I work with many people in the field of spiritual deliverance, and if you discover something I do not know, please write about it, publish it and make your experience available to others in this field. I am not motivated by the desire to be right, but to know the truth, because as Jesus said, "The truth will set you free" **(Jn 8:32)**.

BOOKS BY RITA CABEZAS

ENGLISH

1) A Personal Guide to Daily Spiritual Battle: Prayer for Self-Deliverance

2) Defeating Demonic Principalities: Unveiling Satan's Organizational Hierarchy

3) Healing Hurt Emotions

4) Unmasked: Demons lurking behind psychological symptoms

SPANISH

1) Abuso Emocional

2) Arrebata tu Sanidad

3) Batalla Espiritual

4) ¡Cómo Caíste, Lucero!

5) Conociendo a Dios en el Sufrimiento

6) Conquistemos Territorios

7) Curso de Liberación: Tema Introductorio

8) Depresión: Causas y Manejos

www.ingramcontent.com/pod-product-compliance
Lightning Source LLC
LaVergne TN
LVHW011323080426
835513LV00006B/179